Date Due

POLLY KENT RIDES WEST

In the days of '49

by ROBERT McCULLOCH

Illustrated by
CHARLES HARGENS

JM 13⁸ /ₚ

THE JOHN C. WINSTON COMPANY
Chicago   Philadelphia   Toronto

Polly Kent

To ELEANORE

FOREWORD

Of the forty-seven men who left Rock Island, Illinois, the morning of April fifth, 1849, in a wagon train bound for the gold fields of California, only a few could be drawn into this story.

Little, loosely organized companies like theirs started that year from cities, towns, and villages everywhere throughout the country as soon as the weather would let them travel. Because there was no discipline, and in most cases no close ties of any kind to hold the members together, and because no precautions were taken to safeguard the movement across the plains of the great army of emigrants that massed along the frontier, the long overland journey became a terrible one in which thousands lost their lives.

The Rock Island train was soon split by dissension, and few of its members ever met again. The fate of some of them was never known. But in a diary kept by Charles A. Spring, Jr., a lad of eighteen, who drove a team of cows and oxen, there is mention of the safe arrival at the journey's end of Captain Frezzell, Dr. James Brackett, Otis Dimmock, and Joe Barnett, who had started as the wagon master, and one or two others.

Spring found little gold but returned to Illinois to make two fortunes. One, the Chicago fire swept away. The other he gave with a generous hand—all of it during his lifetime—for the

education in schools and colleges of students in financial need
and for the erection of college buildings.

On his way to *El Dorado* in his youth, he penciled at nearly
every camping place a brief account of the state of the road,
a guess at the distance traveled, and a few words concerning
some adventure, his own or a fellow traveler's. His attention
never strayed far off the road and its problems.

His unpublished diary tells of the river crossings, of the heat,
the storms, the dust, and the hardship. It tells when and where
his own cattle and those of other emigrants were killed or
weakened by the alkaline water they drank, where, along the
way, there was grass and where there was none. Charles Spring's
revealing record of his journey as a forty-niner made it possible
for the writer in this story to string the main incidents on a
true thread of history.

R. W. M.

TABLE OF CONTENTS

ILLUSTRATIONS

(xiii)

I

NO WOMEN!

SOON after dawn a girl in a coonskin cap drove into the mustering camp of a wagon train on the east bank of the Mississippi close to the town of Rock Island.

She sat straight-backed and alert, though she had been driving since midnight. Her single pair of lean buckskin ponies, her stanch little covered wagon, her smoke-colored saddle mare trailing yards behind the ponies were mud-caked and travel-worn. She saw that the big prairie schooners of the train were scattered along beside the river in careless disorder, their covers of new white sheeting spotlessly clean. She noticed too that most of the oxen, standing six or eight to a team ready to take to the road, were logy and fat.

The camp was in confusion. Despite the chill of the spring morning, mothers and wives, fathers, brothers, sisters, and

1

sweethearts were there, anxious for last precious moments of leave taking.

‘ The girl drove with caution, picking her way through the crowd toward a cluster of bearded men in wide-brimmed cloth hats and bright-red flannel shirts, who were standing at, roll call with friends and relatives. Soon she could hear the names read off and the lusty, jubilant answers.

She attracted no attention until a young, black-bearded ox driver suddenly shouted after her:

"Hey, folks! Look! Indian ponies, by hang! An' a light spring wagon! Say, Mister! Think you can git all the way to Californi' in that outfit?"

The girl reined up her ponies sharply and stuck her head around the grimy canvas cover of the forward bow of her rig. For a moment she appeared startled when she saw that all the red-shirted men were staring at her, but she asked quietly:

"Is this train going across the plains?"

"Yes, Miss," someone answered.

"I'd like to join up," she said.

Zenas Rose, the burly, broad-shouldered deputy wagon master who had been reading off the names, dropped his muster book in astonishment. He and the others stood gaping at her.

· The girl put out a foot shod in a boy's sturdy copper-toed shoe and climbed down from the hooded seat. Her long coat, flapping free of her legs, gave the crowd a glimpse of a suit of skins. There was an audible ripple of comment among the wide-skirted women, for the girl's legs were covered with trousers held close below the knees by trappers' leggings.

When she stood facing the men of the train, the coat covered her from chin to ankles and gave her slight, straight figure almost a military bearing. Evidently it had been made to fit a tall man, for the sleeves had been turned back, and it had seen such long service that it had faded to horizon blue. Its big, flat silver buttons and the outdated cut of its cape gave the old garment a dash—something bequeathed by its first owner perhaps—yet it suited the girl.

"Where are the women who are going along?" she asked, turning to glance over the backs of her ponies at the people, apparently of all ages, who were crowding about.

"You won't find 'em!" Rose answered scowlingly. "No women in this outfit!"

Suddenly, a short distance away, a mild-looking, sandy-bearded man in his early forties stood up on a wheel hub. Like most of the men at the roll-call meeting, he wore a red flannel shirt and a wide-brimmed cloth hat. The only difference was that everything he had on was dust-covered and bedraggled, while everything the others wore was clean and new.

"Are you Captain Frezzell, in charge of this train?" he called across the crowd.

"The Captain's down fixin' for us at the ferry," Rose answered. "What you want of him?"

"Has that question of taking women been put to a vote?" the man standing on the hub asked.

Rose reached down to pick up the roll book he had dropped.

"I don't see *you* on this muster roll, Mister," he said.

2

"I reached here only this morning," the man answered. "In February you published for all that wanted to start for California the first week in April to meet here and join up. Your notice didn't say you'd not take women, so I brought my wife and daughter."

Many feminine voices could be heard in stifled exclamation as the crowd grew interested and began to close in.

"Keep off! Don't press up here, folks!" Rose shouted. "Wait till this meeting's over! Only a few minutes more now! Then you can finish up your farewells!" Turning to the anxious stranger he asked, "Where you from?"

"Detroit, Michigan. Brush is my name—Colin Brush. Has the question been put to a vote?"

"Sorry, Brush," Rose answered, "but—no women! That's been understood here ever since we started getting up our train. We met and organized a long while back."

"This is a man's adventure and a man's fitout," a member of the party said frowningly.

"We mean to travel fast," Rose cut in. "Too fast for women-folks! We won't let 'em be hitched onto us! We'll have to make twenty miles a day all through the spring and summer, or winter'll catch us up in the Sierras, or mebby way this side of those mountains, and the whole party'll likely freeze to death or starve."

"Leave your womenfolks behind," Joe Barnett, the wagon master, advised. "If you'll leave 'em here, you can join up with us, provided you're set and ready to start now." He was a reddish man, with merry eyes and a gruff voice.

"I can't leave them!" Brush answered. "Not this far from home! They'll . . ."

"Listen!" Rose interrupted, "this is no women's party! And there's no time to argue! You'll have to find another train!"

"You listen, too, Miss Coonskin Cap!" one of the men shouted. "Better head your horses back where they come from! We don't mean to let no women slow *us* up!"

"That's the fact," Rose stated. "We're in a hurry."

"In a hurry to rush into awful danger!" a sobbing woman protested. "And many a one of you'll never come back!"

Other women began to weep. One laughed. She was very young, very good-looking, and gaily excited.

"Why, they're all coming back—rich! Rich!" she repeated. "Let's give them a good send-off! Don't cry about it!"

"You haven't any brother going way off there, Sarah Lee!" another answered. "If you had, you wouldn't be so pert!"

At that moment a handsome young man who had answered the roll call and was now in the midst of a group of admiring girls, turned toward the sobbing women and sang out in a powerful baritone:

"Oh, Susannah! Don't you cry for me!
I'm off to California with my washbowl on my knee!"

He was not dressed as were the other men of the wagon train. The perfection of his pale, fawn-colored suit and the fineness of his light, wide-brimmed hat made him a conspicuous figure, and called attention to his broad shoulders and his lithe build. His voice was so gay and so full of teasing that the women could not help but smile through their tears.

"We'll come back!" he called to them. "Every last one of us! Don't you worry about that!"

"You'll think of us while you're gone, won't you, Bill?" pleaded one of the girls clinging to his arms. The others about him soon took up the question in chorus.

"Think of you? Every time I drink from this!" He lifted a shining silver canteen out of its leather case, held it up, and pretended to drink. "Even if there's nothing but water in it! And I'm proud of your gift!"

His warm glance flashed from one to another of the girls in the little group of Rock Island's favored daughters, whose newest bonnets and dresses of stiff silk with their enormously wide skirts would set the spring fashions for the town.

"Thanks, Murillo!" Rose turned to Brush. "The first to El Dorado will scoop up the gold! And we're going fast!"

Again there came various comments from the waiting crowd:

"Never do twenty mile a day, Rose!"

"Not twenty-mile-a-day average!"

"Not the hull ways you won't!"

"Yeah, we will—if we ever get started!" someone shouted angrily. "We ought to've been on our way at sunup!"

"Rose," a tall, strong, keen-looking youth said, "we've never had any formal vote on whether we'd take women or not. Let's have one now, so there won't be any question about it."

"All right, Hedges. Fair enough," Zenas Rose assented. "Brush, you've come too late. Anyhow, this is a fitout of *Rock Island men.* Howsomeever, we'll settle that woman question for you. All those for not letting women go with this train say . . . Wait! Hold on a minute! Let's put this so's nobody'll get it wrong. All against letting women go say, 'No!'"

Every man at the roll call shouted his "No" lustily. There was not the least uncertainty about it: women were not to go with this wagon train. For a time the noise of the crowd was stilled, and all looked at the sadly disappointed man on the wagon wheel. Then Zenas Rose grinned. He spoke softly, yet in the momentary hush he was heard to say mockingly:

"All in favor say, 'Aye!' "

"Aye!" cried the girl in the coonskin cap. Hers was the only voice that rang out.

Everyone looked at her. Women craned their necks, and the men who had thundered out their "noes" appeared startled. Rose was too surprised to announce the result of the vote. He gaped at first, then grinned, then guffawed, and at once the crowd burst into laughter.

The girl's eyes flashed in indignation for an instant, but she smiled quickly.

"That's the spirit!" someone offered. "Don't you let 'em down you!"

"Well, Mr. Brush," Zenas Rose said, "nobody can say your daughter don't *want* to go."

"I'm not his daughter!" the girl immediately interposed.

So that he could have a better look at this girl, Murillo moved away from his fair admirers. He was freshly barbered and beardless. His red silk handkerchief which was knotted about his neck with artful carelessness was of a pattern and of a shade of red that only the East Indies were producing at the time for expensive trade. He spoke with gallant courtesy, sweeping off his hat with a wide flourish.

The girl looked at him with a catch of her breath. With his easy air of confidence and his fascinating grace, he brought to mind her father, who had been the dashing hero of her childhood and all her later years. She thought that her father, if he were living and with her now, would find something of his own adventurous spirit in this handsome young Murillo.

"Who are you then?" Murillo asked. "Who are you, if we may be so bold? And where are you from?"

"It was gosh awful thoughtful of you, Bill, edgin' that 'we' in!" a man in the crowd shouted. "Even us old codgers clean out o' the runnin' want to know, too!"

"I'm Polly Kent," the girl answered in momentary embarrassment. "I'm from the Wabash River, down below Terre Haute."

"Where are your menfolks, Miss Kent?" Brush called to her. "I want to join up with them! My wagon's 'The Wolverene,' out yonder on the edge of the camp."

The girl drew her lips together and lifted her head. "I haven't any menfolks," she answered. "I'm making the trip alone."

A brief silence, in which everyone gazed at her again in astonishment, was followed by murmurs of disbelief and a buzz of talk among the women.

"Well, that beats all!" Brush exclaimed.

Then a tipsy youth approached the girl and stood directly in front of her. "Well, Miss Terry Hut," he said, loud enough for all to hear, "we know blame well no decent woman's headin' out alone on this kind of a ja'nt."

He had hardly finished speaking when she smacked him hard in the face.

"Good fer you, sis!" came a shrill feminine voice from far off in the crowd. "Slap 'im agin fer good count!"

But Polly Kent darted up to the seat of her light spring wagon. With movements swift and sure she brought down a rifle that hung under the shelter of the cover. Without moving from the seat, she swung the muzzle toward the drunken man before anyone could reach him. Her eyes were blazing.

Several members of the wagon train, who had started toward the fellow threateningly, stopped in surprise and stood looking up at her.

"You heard me say *I* was going, didn't you, Mister?" she asked.

"Put up your rifle, please, Miss," young Hedges urged gently.

"Say!" cried the tipsy youth in alarm. "Be careful o' that gun! Take a joke, can't you? I didn't mean nothin' pussonel!"

"Don't kill him, sis!" warned the shrill-voiced woman. "He aint wu'th the trouble a bullet'd make fer you!"

"The lady out yonder's right!" As Zenas Rose spoke, he moved quickly between the girl and the man her rifle was covering and knocked him down. "Better leave the rifle where it is," he said. "And now, with Gale Hedges hustling him out of camp, we've settled that score for you."

"Sakes alive!" the girl exclaimed. "You're all so hard set against women I didn't know whether you'd settle it or not. I can take care of myself!"

"Me, I'm layin' odds she kin!" exclaimed a grizzled man near by. He paused to grin at Rose, whose cheeks were growing red as he glared. "I'm layin' you gay young coots eagles to coppers she kin take care o' herself. Blamed good-lookin', too, an' smart as a whip!"

"I'm obliged to you just the same, Mr. Rose," the girl said, ignoring the comment about herself, "you, and that Mr. Hedges." Sliding her rifle back into the looped straps inside the wagon cover, she added slowly, "But I should think that a few decent women would be of more help to you crossing the plains than any men like that."

"He don't belong in this train!" several promptly told her.

"No, nor in any other train," one shouted. "He'd rather hunt liquor than gold!"

"But not takin' any womenfolks is a mighty bad mistake, Zenas," the distant shrill voice cut in, "as I been tellin' you all along! The Mormons took 'em!"

"Mercy save us!" another woman burst out. "Aunt Rinthy spoke the truth! They took a-plenty!"

"So did the folks that struck fer Oregon last year!" Aunt Rinthy added. "An' I bet word'll come how they got through safe, too!"

The crowd, which was in a high-strung mood, laughed at this. When there was quiet, Brush added gravely, "Come along, Miss, and meet my wife and daughter."

At that moment a crisp, dark man, slender, rather impressive, and wearing a neatly trimmed black beard, stood up on the tongue of an ox wagon and spoke in a voice that carried far.

"You must remember," he began, "that in both those migrations, the men were going out to make homes for their families, so, of course, they took their women with them—their women and their children, their plows, and even their household goods. For that very reason, they traveled slowly.

"But this is different; it's a race for gold! A mad race—and the devil take the hindmost! The first to cross the plains will be the first to come back rich!"

Excited cries drowned his voice. In a moment he shouted, "We mean to be among the first to reach the gold fields!"

At the end of the cheer that greeted this declaration, a woman cried, "You can't make us believe that, Doctor Brackett! We know that many a one of you won't ever come back!"

"Hush, Caroline!" the gaily excited Sarah Lee broke in. "You'll make me laugh again!"

"Some of you'll never get halfway across the plains!" the woman persisted. "Some of you'll get . . . some of you'll . . ." Suddenly she broke into tears, and several women about her also began to sob.

"Hurry it, Zenas! Better get started before the rest of the women catch hysterics!" Doctor Brackett said, as he disappeared from the wagon tongue.

"I want to say one thing more!" Rose shouted. "The trouble with you women is that you've heard only a strong party can fight the Indians off, and you're worried. Well, we're a strong party! Don't you forget that! Forty-seven men with plenty of guns and powder and lead! Forty-seven men, seventeen wagons, a hundred and eight oxen, and seven cows. And say! All the way out to St. Joe we'll do twenty-five miles a day! And we'll . . ." He held up his hand. "Here's Captain Frezzell!"

Frezzell, an alert, pleasant-mannered man, a former steamboat captain, looked about at the members of the party for a moment. "Keep your water barrels filled," he said. "Get that habit fixed. And listen, you fellows who joined late. A lot, like us, may head out through St. Joe. Right here, right now's your last chance to check your supply lists. We'll likely find St. Joe clean sold out of foodstuffs, and prices will be sky-high. No towns, no settlers out beyond there, remember, no chance to buy. So don't a one of you leave your list shy of anything your life may depend on four or five months from now. All right, Joe!"

"Just a minute there! Just a minute!" A very spry, brusque man hopped up on the wagon tongue from which Doctor Brackett had spoken, and lifted a hand to gain attention.

"Wait, all!" Frezzell shouted. "Wait and hear what Captain John Wilson's got to say!"

The members of the company, who had begun to move away toward their teams, paused to listen.

"You boys can't head west out of Rock Island without you cross the Mississippi, the biggest river you'll meet up with anywheres, thank God!" Wilson said. "Well, everybody knows I run the Rock Island ferry. I wish I could ferry this train at

every creek and river twixt hither and yon. But my boat's
too big to be drug over the plains, so I'm set to tell you I'm
goin' to put you all over on the I'way side—men, oxen, and
big prairie schooners—free of charge!"

Cheers greeted this announcement.

"What's the toll going to be per wagonload of gold coming
back?" Bill Murillo shouted.

"You go get the gold, boys! Time you're back, I'll mebby
have that toll figgered out!"

Wilson stepped down, and there was a moment of renewed
cheering.

"Thanks, Captain!" Frezzell said. "Speaking for all—men,
steers, and big prairie schooners—thanks! Now every driver
to his wagon! The crossing will take quite a spell; so you home
folks better drift down to the ferry with us. All right, boys,
get started!"

Someone began to sing the gold seekers' version of "Oh,
Susannah!" the most popular song of the time. The crowd
quickly took it up:

> "I soon shall be in mining camps,
> And then I'll look around,
> And when I see the gold dust there,
> I'll pick it off the ground.

> "I'll scrape the mountains clean, old girl,
> I'll drain the rivers dry;
> I'm off to California,
> Susannah, don't you cry!

> "Oh, Susannah! Don't you cry for me!
> I'm off to California with my washbowl on my knee!"

The young boys who had been sitting importantly on the seats in the covered wagons now climbed down reluctantly, and gave over their places to their older brothers or to their fathers.

Half the dogs of the town had followed the crowd to camp, and they set to barking as the oxen started and the heavy wheels began to turn. Above all the hubbub, men could be heard shouting at their teams and at one another, and everywhere the women who walked beside the wagons were weeping.

II

THE ROAD'S FREE!

EUSEBIA BRUSH, waiting beside her wagon, could see the crowd dispersing. She could hear men calling, hear the answering voices of women, the rumble of wheels, and the creaking of gear as the train began to form. She heard a girl who was passing say:

"Freddie, that's the wife of the man from Detroit. See the name 'The Wolverene,' on the wagon?"

"Mebby!" the youth who was with the girl answered.

Mrs. Brush saw that this fellow was wearing all the trappings of a gold seeker. She knew that in every town, village, and city the country over, a man setting out for California by ship or by wagon was expected to wear tucked-in trousers, a belt with knife and pistol, a flannel shirt, a wide soft hat, and a beard. This youth's beard was so blond and scant and silken that it could hardly be noticed.

15

"Do you reckon she'll give up going now?" asked the girl.
"Mebby."

Mrs. Brush, as she listened to them, began to look around for her husband. Because she did not see him, she grew anxious. She saw people hurrying everywhere. Above the noise of the entraining, above the outcries and clamor, she heard a man shouting:

"Wagon number four! Number four!"

As another couple passed, she heard the girl ask:

"Lester, why does Joe Barnett call the men by number? Doesn't he know all of you by name?"

"Five next!" came the voice of the wagon master. "Swing lively!"

"The numbers are the places in the line," answered a beardless boy standing beside the girl. "They drew for them yesterday, before I bought Lem Crandall's interest in a wagon."

"What's your number?"

"Seventeen."

"Oh, that's fine!"

"Fine? To be the last in the train? Fine to have to take the whole party's dust for two thousand miles?"

"But, Lester!" the girl faltered, "it lets you be with *me* a—just a little while longer! Uh! huh! huh! you know there's dust—I mean grass—nothing but grass on the plains!" She moved away sobbing.

"Hush up! Hush up!" her companion kept repeating as they passed out of Mrs. Brush's hearing.

Then the woman who was waiting for her husband saw him come slowly around his team of cows and oxen.

"What is it?" she said quickly. "What is it, Colin? Is there any trouble?"

"Sebie," Brush answered, "they won't let us join this train, either."

"Why won't they?" she questioned breathlessly. "You mean . . . Tell me!"

"Not taking any women."

The two stood looking at each other.

"But . . . then, are we going? Durst we? With Ann? You know you said this was our last chance, Colin." She turned to look toward a slim young girl who was watching the wagons swing into their allotted places and move off in an ever-lengthening line toward the ferry landing. "Honey! Come here, dear!" the woman called.

"Don't bother her," Brush cautioned. "Don't set Ann to worrying. We can't go back, Eusebia. You know very well we've burned our bridges."

"No, we can't go back," Eusebia agreed.

"But," her husband took up quickly, "we can stop and settle down on prairie land anywhere this side of the Missouri River, or even a ways beyond, if it comes to that. And right on out to the last jumping-off place, we'll keep on looking for a train we *can* travel with—one that *is* taking women."

"But, Colin, you'll not want land. A boat builder should stay near water, a river or . . ."

She did not say any more, for she could see that, quiet as he was, the fever of adventure was burning in him as he watched the departing train. And she was sure that she and Ann would go on and on with him all the way to California.

"See this girl coming?" he said presently. "She wanted to go with them, too."

Polly Kent drove carefully through the crowd that was trailing off with the wagons. She drew up and turned appraising eyes on the woman who, like herself, had been excluded from the departing train.

"You still think of going?" Brush asked her.

"Certainly!" the girl exclaimed, looking at him in astonishment. Then she laughed, "Oh, not with that Rock Island outfit, Mr. Brush," she added.

"Sebie," said Brush, turning to his wife, "this is Polly Kent, from Terre Haute. She's going to California alone."

"Mercy me!" Eusebia Brush exclaimed. "Why, you don't mean that you . . .?"

"What say we make one party?" her husband suggested. "Three women and one man—all going together?"

"You spunky thing!" the woman cried, reaching out both hands to the girl eagerly.

All in one movement Polly came off the seat and over the wheel to the ground.

"But you, . . ." Mrs. Brush stared at her unbelievingly. "You can't mean all by yourself?"

"I've heard so much about the plains and the mountains, Mrs. Brush, that it won't seem to me like a strange country out there," Polly replied. "I feel as if I'll know every single mile of the way."

"No tears now, Sebie!" Brush warned good-naturedly. "There, there, no blubbering!"

"But to think of 'er starting out alone!" The plump, kindly matron grimaced painfully in her effort to keep back the tears. "And such a little wagon! Colin, you see to it that she has enough supplies and everything! You see to that, whether she's willing to join us or not!" She turned to the girl. "You listen to him!" she urged. "He's very forethoughted."

"I'm more than willing," the girl assured the two promptly. "I'll be glad to join up. With my ponies, I could go faster than you can. Your oxen and cows will travel slowly, but if we start together, I'll stick with you the whole way. I'll give you my hand on that. And I'll not be a burden."

"You'll be such a comfort to Ann and me!" The woman was almost in tears again.

"All right," Brush replied, "that's an agreement. And we'll make it somehow. We'll make it!" His eyes squinted, and he stood for a moment thinking. "We'll find some train, never fear, before we go far. And now we'll be moving along. We'll have to go into the town. Rock Island's where I'll have to lay in all we'll need for the whole of the rest of the journey. Get into the wagon, Sebie."

"We'll traipse along," his wife answered. "I want to talk to her—to Polly. She's going to be right with us all the time!"

Brush started his oxen. The girl turned her ponies, clicked at them, and they fell in behind the heavy wagon.

3

"Number ten!" Barnett shouted. "Close up, ten! Number eleven! Keep moving!"

"Come, Daughter!" Brush called.

"Hurry, Ann!" the mother added, as she and Polly walked on together.

The slim young girl who came running had tow-colored hair hanging in braids, and skin that was still fair after many days of travel. When she caught up with them, Eusebia said:

"Here's Ann, our little one."

Polly turned around, and the younger girl looked into blue, blue eyes that startled her with their sparkle. She saw a smoothly modeled face with a thin, fine nose, a straight, closed mouth, and eyebrows that penciled off into wings, blue-black like the hair that edged down from under the coonskin cap.

"Honey, we've found the kind of company you've wanted," Eusebia said. "Her name's Polly Kent. She was expecting to go with the Rock Island train, too, but they won't take women."

"Not any, Mother? Not us?" the girl asked in alarm.

"No, only men. So we've decided to go together."

The girls, who were still looking at each other, smiled.

"How many are there in your party?" the younger one inquired.

"One," Polly answered.

"Oh!" came in a slow and long-drawn-out sound from Ann.

"How old are you?" Mrs. Brush asked suddenly, turning to Polly.

"Nineteen," Polly told her.

"Number fifteen!" This time the wagon master's voice seemed to come from far behind them.

They had taken a short-cut, and the jumbled sounds of preparation for the river crossing came up to them from the ferry. Here and there men again were singing "Oh, Susannah!"

"Mr. Brush!" Gale Hedges called. "Come this way!"

Brush swung in and halted his oxen close to where the crowd was now re-forming. Polly's ponies stopped of their own accord.

"Keiēta!" the girl called. "Keiēta!"

With that, Polly's smoke-colored saddle mare trotted up obediently and stood beside her.

"Some of you women go head off that fool girl from Terre Haute!" Zenas Rose shouted, so that Polly and those around her could hear. "Head her back toward the Wabash where she belongs!"

"You just try that, Zenas!" It was Aunt Rinthy's sharp, high voice that called. "I got all I kin do to keep from strikin' right out along with 'er, old as I be!"

"Mr. Brush," Hedges said, "we're all traveling light out to St. Joe, so as to make fast time on that part of the trip. Brackett's starting down river today to buy our supplies for us in St. Louis. He's to ship them up to St. Joe and have them there ahead of us. If you're going on from here, he can buy all your stuff, too, and send it up along with ours. I guess we owe you that much because of the notice we printed."

"That's a kind suggestion," Brush answered and looked at his wife.

"Better to travel as light as you can that far. We'll make time by it, and we'll keep our cattle fit for the long, hard journey beyond the Missouri. Need anything?"

"I'll need everything from there on—everything in the food line," Brush told him. "I meant to stock up heavy here at Rock Island."

"Then why not follow along after us as far as St. Joe, and load up when the wagon train does?"

"Well," Brush replied, glancing again at his wife, "it certainly would be the better way."

Mrs. Brush knew that he was trying to avoid making her feel he would decide anything so important as this without her consent. She drew a deep breath, wet her lips, looked at Polly Kent, then said:

"Whatever happens, Colin, we can use the food. Tell him what you want."

"Have you a list ready?" Hedges looked the crowd over. "You'll find Brackett still around somewhere. But I don't know when the down-river boat's due to leave, so you'd better not delay."

"I'll get it," Brush answered quickly. As he climbed into his wagon, he called over his shoulder, "How are *you* fixed, Miss?"

"Never mind her!" Rose interposed hurriedly.

"Want I should put you a list in with mine?" Brush asked again.

"We don't buy anything for her!" Rose replied sharply. "We'll not have 'er trailing close to us for favors!"

"She's a member of our party!" Mrs. Brush informed him severely.

"No matter! Hey, Brackett!" he shouted, "this man Brush wants to see you! There he is, Brush, over yonder!"

"Wait a minute, Zenas!" Gale Hedges said quickly. "Getting supplies for her is something Brackett can decide for himself. Did our published notice bring you up this far out of your way, Miss Kent?"

"No, I had to come north before I was ready to start," Polly answered. "And I never heard of your notice until today, Mr. Hedges. It wouldn't have brought me here if I had. There are too many other trains. They start out from every town."

"Any of 'em taking women?" Rose broke in.

"None that I've heard of," Polly admitted.

"What did I tell you!" Rose cried.

"Mercy me!" exclaimed Mrs. Brush.

"But that's what we've heard ever since we left home, Sebie," her husband reminded her soothingly. He added, turning toward the two men, "I thought, from your notice, that we might be lucky and join on."

"I'm certainly not encouraging Miss Kent to go," Hedges said. "I'd turn her back if I could."

"You can't!" Polly assured him.

"All right! The road's free!" Rose snapped at her. "But you'll turn back once you get out yonder and see what's ahead of you, young lady!"

"Well," Hedges admitted, "if she's bent on going, and she seems to be, I'm for the doctor's buying her goods for her."

"Gale," the other man answered angrily, "we haven't got a minute to waste on her! Just because she happens to be young and halfway good looking . . ."

"Don't quarrel!" Polly interrupted. "There's nothing I wish to buy. I started from home with everything I need."

"Not everything!" Mrs. Brush gazed at her wide-eyed. "Oh, but you must let Colin check over with you to be sure."

"I started with everything I'll need except the game to be had along the way. There's nothing I want, Mrs. Brush, really."

"Game!" Rose exclaimed contemptuously.

"Think a minute," Brush urged. He evidently shared his wife's fear that Polly was not well supplied. "It's the last chance, you know, and I have to hurry to catch Doctor Brackett. You're sure? All right." Without further conversation, he hastened away.

"Game!" Rose repeated. "Who do you think'll get game for you, I'd like to know?"

"If you'd seen the hundreds of skins drying on our cabin walls at home, you'd not ask that," Polly answered. "I've grown up with a rifle."

"Well," Rose returned, "if there was no one at home able to stop you, then I suppose we can't."

Polly gave him no answer, but she turned to Mrs. Brush.

"There wasn't anyone at home to stop me," she said. "There were only the two of us—Father and I. My mother died when I was a child, and when Father was off on his long absences, I was left with the French Sisters of Providence at the Mission

of Saint Mary-of-the-Woods, near the Wabash. Right after
word came of the finding of gold in California, he was at home.
It was there that he died."

"But what's troubling me most," Hedges told her, "is that
you're starting with nothing but ponies. Doctor Brackett, and
his partner, Dimmock, have a little outfit like yours; but the
rest of us are going to haul their supplies, so they can scout
ahead for feed and camping places for us."

The girl saw that he was much concerned.

"My father had planned to use ponies," she answered. "If
he had been going alone, he would not have taken a wagon
at all, only pack animals. But with me along, he said the wagon
would be more convenient. He knew the far west country—
the Rockies and beyond. He was with Bonneville."

Hedges looked at her in a kind of awe, and repeated slowly,
"Bonneville! With Captain Bonneville?"

"No wonder she's going!" Mrs. Brush exclaimed, feeling
sudden confidence in the girl. "She's got adventure in her
blood!"

"Well!" Hedges still gazed at Polly. "No one in our party's
ever even talked to anybody that's been across the Rocky
Mountains. What did your father think about oxen?"

"He wouldn't use them," she answered. "Captain Bonneville
had some at the start."

"Why not? Why wouldn't your father use 'em?" a woman
who had been listening broke in.

Polly glanced at her, but continued to speak to Hedges.
"He said they'd probably get through if they were looked

after properly. But my three ponies were bred and raised on the plains. They can haul the wagon, carry pack or saddle, travel fast, and fend for themselves in any kind of country where other Indian ponies can.

"They fare better than cattle do. They are more apt to keep away from alkali water. Father wouldn't drive oxen because they travel with their noses so close to the ground that they breathe in the alkali dust and then they sicken and die. They have to be watched and looked after carefully."

"Oh, dear! Oh, dear!" cried Mrs. Brush. "And here we have six oxen and two cows! Why didn't we know that? Why didn't we?"

"O Freddie! You hear that? Freddie Dascomb!" cried the woman who had asked the question a moment before. "You're not going! Not with them oxen! Somebody holler to 'im!" She began to run about, weeping and calling frantically.

"The silly thing!" Sarah Lee exclaimed. "He'll be back— rich! They all will! And how their womenfolks are taking on!"

"Look, Sarah!" piped up a feminine voice maliciously. "Your brother's calling you. I didn't know he was going!"

"Going? Lester? Where?" Sarah's last question rose to a thin wail. "Lester Lee!" she cried. "Why are you dressed like that?"

"Hush up! Hush up! I've been hunting for you everywhere!" answered the beardless boy who had passed Eusebia's wagon at the time of the entraining. "Lucky me!" he exulted. "Lem Crandall's ma had a dream last night of him dying of thirst in the desert, so this morning he sold me his share in the wagon he owned with Preston. Aunt Rinthy lent me the money!"

"O Lester! Lester Lee! O Lester!" shrieked Sarah. "No, you're not going!" She threw her arms about him and clung to him. "I'll not let you go! I'll not let you!"

"Makes a difference when it's folks of your own, I'd say!" the same malicious voice taunted. " 'Pears like!"

Down at the river Captain Wilson shouted from the end of the ferryboat, "Move back, everybody! Off the landing, or you'll be trompled on! Say, Barnett, it looks from here like some of your town boys never drove oxen before. I don't want my boat stove in!"

"I'll get their teams aboard," the wagon master answered.

"Hey, Wilson, don't let none o' them cussed dogs on the boat!" someone shouted. "We can't have no dogs foller us onto the plains, an' it looks like the whole train's pestered with 'em!"

"You home folks grab your dogs!" Wilson called out. "All right, Captain Frezzell! Start off your train for points west! One fitout, Captain, will be all the load we can take at a crossing."

The chatter of the crowd was suddenly lost in a thunderous rumble, as the first of the big covered wagons rolled onto the ferry, bound for the land of gold.

III

LAST AT THE FERRY

THE ox train followed the river southward in a muddy road after crossing the ferry, and spent the night so near the town that a party of young men and women rode out on horseback to have tea with friends at the camp.

Next morning there was torrential rain. Because nearly every new schooner hood consisted of a single layer of unbleached sheeting which leaked badly where the cloth touched the bows, the men had to shift and reshift the contents of the wagons in vain efforts to keep the food and bedding dry.

Within an hour after entraining, they were all trudging beside their teams in the downpour so as to lighten the loads of the laboring cattle. The Brushes and Polly had camped beyond them, and thus were able to keep ahead that day.

At Duck Creek the members of the main party halted again
to save the tender necks of their oxen, which were becoming
galled. A few miles north of this camping place they passed
thirty-odd mule teams from South Bend, Indiana, stuck deep
in the mud. Between these two trains a race for the lead began
which soon caused a bitter clash.

· · The men of both companies, like all the countless thousands
then mustering or on their overland way to California, with
only vague forewarnings of the hardship and danger awaiting
them, feared most of all that when they reached the mining
fields, others ahead of them would have all the gold. In their
feverish haste, they grew anxious and angry over the slightest
delay. They were bent on getting a place in the lead and
holding it all the way to the journey's end.

Colin Brush, wise to road conditions since his trip from
Detroit, refused to wear his animals down in the race with the
mules. Walking beside them in the beating rain, he never let
them quicken their plodding pace, and he rested them frequently. Days before, he had spread thick duck over the first
thin sheeting of his wagon hood, and heavy canvas over that,
so Ann and Sebie could ride in comfort and keep dry in any
kind of weather. He had also fastened inside the hood at the
back of his wagon a strong, neatly made lidded box with a
toilet seat under the lid and overhanging the road. Out against
the wagon bed, his water barrel was firmly set above the
space between the wheels on the side where he now trudged
along. Though the other oxen kept the lead for hours, then
lost it, then regained it, his were not hurried.

Polly rode well sheltered, keeping close behind the Brushes. She camped with them again beyond the ox train's halting place, and with them took to the road the next morning before the heavy schooners passed, to leave it deeply rutted. All the ox teams were trailing the South Bend party the next afternoon at Muscatine. There both trains swung west from the Mississippi, heading out toward the fork of the Cedar and the Iowa rivers, some twenty-five miles away. Soon the oxen moved into the lead, but before evening the mules passed them. Thereafter, whenever the road was sandy, the mule drivers whipped their animals to a trot and went by whooping. Where there was deep mud, the men from Rock Island whooped and yelled as they left the mules behind.

Toward sundown of the following day, on a piece of good, rapidly drying road near the confluence of the Cedar and the Iowa, the mules trotted past the oxen in time to be first at the ferry.

While the last of the Rock Island wagons were lining up behind the other train to await their turn at the crossing, Polly Kent came riding back from the landing on one of her ponies. Another pony, without lead rope or bridle, followed, bearing a pack in which were three sacks of corn.

That morning, before Captain Frezzell could get his party started, Polly had driven past in her light rig, which was now standing beside the road at the far end of the line where Brush was unyoking his tired cattle.

"Lady rides astride, huh!" someone shouted derisively as she passed.

"That your interestin' little buggy an' what's in it camped back yonder, lady?" a man named Tasker, of the South Bend outfit, called to her.

"That's my wagon," Polly called back.

"You part o' the Rock Island train?" Tasker asked.

"No," she answered. "The party I'm with is following along behind."

"Party that sends a lady out scoutin' after corn with a pack pony's a mighty little outfit, I'd say! Ain't you feared somebody'll steal that load o' yourn? How'd you like to make a trade?"

At that moment Captain Frezzell and several others came forward in search of the South Bend captain. Gale Hedges, who was one of them, said to Polly:

"How's the outlook ahead? Any chance to buy feed?"

"There's some—but not much—on the other side of the ferry, Mr. Hedges," she told him. "And there's a place just up the stream where you can drive your cattle in to drink."

"You drive your cattle in down below, an' don't rile up the stream fer our mules!" Tasker ordered.

"We'll water where we please!" Zenas Rose answered angrily.

"Easy now, Zenas!" the captain warned. "I'm captain of this train, Mister, and my name's Frezzell."

"Mine's Webb Tasker."

"We've got a light spring wagon we want to drive across after feed for the morning. Where's your captain, Tasker?"

"No wagon goes onto this ferry, Frezzell, till every last one o' ours rolls off on the other side," Tasker answered. "We've talked it over. No need fer you to bother the captain. That's settled."

"But we've got to have feed for our stock while your train's crossing, and that will take the better part of tomorrow."

"Try to git it!" Tasker replied menacingly.

Polly had stopped to listen. "Don't let them start a quarrel, Mr. Hedges," she urged in a low voice. "The landing on the other side is so bad after all the rain that you couldn't get a wagon back after dark, anyway. The ferryman says he'll not dare to run at night till he gets the new ferryboat he's expecting."

"That can't be right!" exclaimed Captain Frezzell, who had overheard the conversation. "But hurry back, Hedges, and warn the men to feed light tonight. Meanwhile I'll look into this."

"Where is Mr. Murillo?" Polly asked Gale Hedges, as he walked back beside her pony. "I haven't seen him since we started. I've thought of something that he may be able to carry through for us."

"What is it?" Hedges asked. "Bill's not with us."

The girl glanced at him in surprise and disappointment. She wondered why Murillo had not come, but she did not ask. Hedges, too, was silent.

"Where's your captain?" they heard Frezzell call out. "We'll have to get feed over to our stock before your train is out of the way."

And they heard Tasker answer, "You should o' beat us to the ferry!" while behind them several men laughed.

"More than two dozen trains have passed here," Polly said to Hedges.

"Two dozen!" he exclaimed. "And we thought we'd be about the first to start from anywhere! That's bad business, Miss Kent. We haven't gone sixty miles—much less the hundred twenty-five we'd counted on—in the five days since we set out. With heavily loaded wagons, we hardly could have made it at all during this muddy spell. And now, with the oxen on scant feed, we'll be delayed a whole day more while this other train is being ferried over."

"I hope you'll warn your men to drive the oxen downstream to water, and not cause trouble," Polly said.

"You would, of course! That's the woman of it!" Hedges answered, a note of scorn in his voice. By this time they had left the South Bend wagons behind them, and he called to some Rock Island men they were passing, "Boys, you'd better take your rifles along. There's a good place upstream to water the steers, but the party ahead's honing for trouble."

"Wait, please!" Polly stopped her pony and dismounted. Stepping close to Hedges, she said, "The ferryman has a larger boat coming up the river tomorrow—due up then. From a few words he dropped, I think he'd be willing to sell this one any time. If you owned it, your train could cross ahead of the South Bend teams."

"They wouldn't let us. The mule train has the road blocked right down to the landing," Hedges answered. "It wouldn't do us any good to buy the boat. That outfit would give us a battle, and we couldn't get past them to use the ferry ahead of them."

"The ferry is just an old flatboat attached by pulleys to a cable that's stretched from bank to bank," Polly told him. "The current pushes the boat back and forth." She paused a moment while she studied Hedges, for she was not at all certain he was the man to take up the suggestion she wished to make. At last, however, she continued, "If you drive the oxen downstream, the South Bend people will think you are mighty timid—the whole lot of you."

"Well, they'd have a right to think so!" Hedges answered.

"And if they should think so," the girl ventured, "they'd not keep watch of us during the night—either of us or of the ferry."

"I don't see any point in that." The young fellow began to look at her intently. "You've got something else on your mind, haven't you?"

"Yes," Polly answered promptly. "If Mr. Brush and I go in with you men and buy the boat that's now in use, we can throw off its pulley lines during the night and let it float down the river about a mile to where the crossing used to be. Then we can turn our wagons around, double back to the old road that leads down there, and begin to ferry across first thing in the morning."

"Gehosiphat!" Hedges cried. "You sure of that?"

"The ferryman told me. When he said he didn't know what he'd do with the old boat after the new one came tomorrow, I asked him a lot of questions. You see, after traveling that last long stretch of sandy road, I was afraid the mule train would get here first."

"Gehosiphat! We'd avoid a whole day's delay! Well, I'm glad you went scouting ahead, Miss Kent. We should have sent our own spring wagon out."

"But if we do buy the boat and head back to the ferry . . ."

"Well?"

"Well, Mr. Brush, who is now the last in the line, would then be first, and I think he should be allowed to cross first, don't you?"

"That's fair enough." Hedges grinned at her. "You know how to bargain, don't you?" He turned to the men who were rounding up the oxen. "Put up your guns, boys," he said cautiously. "Let's water the cattle downstream instead. Miss Terry Hut, here, has a better idea than mine was."

"Not this evening, thank you!" answered Lester Lee, who had taken down his rifle. "If the Hoosiers up front are honing for trouble, we'll give it to 'em!"

"Right you are, Lester!" Freddie Dascomb contributed.

"What is her idea?" an older man inquired.

"We'll put that up to Captain Frezzell, first of all," Hedges answered. "Hold the cattle back for a while. He's coming now."

The captain, Zenas Rose, and three others who had gone forward with him to talk to the men of the mule train, were returning troubled and angry.

"Well, they mean to stand by what that fellow Tasker said!" the captain informed the group. "No feed comes back for our stock till they all get across. Won't even let an empty wagon of ours go over tomorrow."

4

"I'd like to see 'em try that!" Zenas Rose blustered.

"You heard what they said, Zenas! They're agreed on that. Had it all figgered out. And I want to tell you the hole they're putting us in is a mighty bad one!"

"They said it, all right!" Rose answered. "But we'll see about that! There's no feed left for a good eight miles behind us. While the other trains that went through were waiting here at the ferry, they sent back wagons along the road and cleaned it all up. All right! This girl says there's a little ahead. We'll get it!"

"But this South Bend outfit'll grab all that," Joe Barnett warned.

"I heard you say you'd have to have hay, Mr. Barnett, so I bought a small stack from the farmer across the river for eleven dollars," Polly said. "I paid him three dollars down on it."

"Good business, Miss!" Barnett took off his hat to her, then slapped it back on his head. "Wait! Here's your three dollars! We're mighty much obliged to you!"

"We'll get men across the river tonight if we have to swim!" Rose declared. "And, boys, we'll hold that stack against this band of Benders if their mules starve! They've got to have hay to head on with from here!"

"We may not have to do that," Hedges said. "Let's call a council of war, Captain. Miss Kent here tells me we can probably buy the ferryboat if we go about it cautiously. Buy it and float it a mile down the river tonight to where the old crossing used to be, double back our wagons to the old road that runs down there, and start getting our train over tomorrow at daylight."

The men who had crowded up to listen became excited.

"She holds that she and Brush must be the first to cross," Hedges added.

"After your empty wagon goes over for feed for your cattle, of course," Polly amended.

"This time, by hang, I vote for Miss Terry Hut!" one of the men shouted.

"Don't get to yelling!" Frezzell cautioned in a whisper. "Want to warn those fellows up ahead that we're cooking up something against them?"

"And Miss Kent thinks we'd do well to have our cattle watered downstream," Hedges said softly, "to make the South Benders think, after the threats they made, that we're a party of scared rabbits, so they won't feel called on to keep watch at that ferry tonight."

The men began to talk in low voices and to dance about.

"Hush! Hush! Hush!" Frezzell kept repeating. "Don't make 'em think we're hatching up anything here! All right now, keep quiet! This young lady and Brush go across first, provided it turns out she's right about the boat, and we can buy it. But now every man keeps his mouth shut! Drive the cattle down the stream! Take all the guff any South Bender wants to give you! Take it meek and sorrowful, with no back talk. First off, let each wagon authorize a man to drift back to the end of the line out of earshot and bring money along. We'll see what we can do about this little matter."

"Hey, Lester," Freddie Dascomb called softly. "Let's be nice and hang up our rifles."

"Mine's up, Freddie," Lester answered. "I'll not rile any ruction tonight if I have to tote water to these horned hosses of ours in my boots."

"I'm going right with you now, Miss Kent," Frezzell decided, falling in beside the girl. "Come on, Hedges, you and Barnett and Zenas. I suppose you followed that back road down to the old ferry crossing, didn't you, young lady, so's to be sure that we can make it with the wagons?"

"No," Polly answered, "but I'll be glad to ride down and . . ."

"I'll do that!" Barnett broke in. "You say we can throw off the pulley lines. But how about that cable line that's strung across the river?"

"The ferryman won't sell that—Sebastian, they call him. He wants the cable for his new boat when it comes up. It's a heavy cable that he bought on purpose."

"Then we'll have to pole across," Frezzell said. "And we'll need poles."

"I'll look out for them," Barnett promised quickly.

"You'll find plenty down along the stream," Polly informed the men. "I rode down on the other side to see how the road over there is. It's good." She held out a string of gray squirrels she had thrown up on the load of corn before starting back on the ferry.

"Here, Mrs. Brush," she called. "I've an extra mess for you."

"Wherever did you get 'em, child?" Eusebia exclaimed.

."The woods along the river are full of them," Polly told her. "They seem to be migrating: all going west with the covered wagons." She laughed. "They do migrate sometimes."

"Well, that's some of the game Polly told you about back there in Rock Island, Mr. Rose," the other woman said, pleased to get in a little dig at him.

"And every danged one shot in the head!" Joe Barnett looked at the girl in surprise. "I'd say you know how to use a rifle, Miss! That's what I call mighty good . . ."

"Let's get down to business about this boat!" Rose interrupted in a sour tone. "Here come the boys."

Several men came hurrying up. "It's buy the boat!" one of them said. "Every partner in every wagon's for it. But what's it going to cost?"

"Two, three hundred dollars—mebby more," Frezzell answered. "We'll find that out. But we can go high if we have to; we've got to get across."

"Oh, not so much as two hundred dollars!" Polly protested.

"Well, I'd like to be counted in," Brush said.

"You and the girl both, of course," Frezzell assured him.

"Why the regular ferry charge would be only thirty-four dollars and eighty-five cents," Polly stated. "Nineteen wagons counting all of us, at thirty cents each. That's five dollars and seventy cents. A hundred thirty-three animals, at twenty cents, is twenty-six sixty, and fifty-one persons, at five cents, is two fifty-five. Mr. Sebastian feels sure that his new ferry will be up tomorrow. Why, I think he ought to be glad to sell that old flatboat for forty or fifty dollars."

"Me, too!" young Lee chimed in. "That's how I figgered it."

"No time for jokes now, Lester," Frezzell warned brusquely. "What say we appoint a committee to see the ferryman?"

"We'll be satisfied if you and Barnett handle that, Captain," one of the men suggested.

"Look out! Mule skinners coming!" Barnett warned softly.

"Careful now! All right, we'll see the ferryman," the captain whispered. Aloud, he said as a dozen South Bend men came up, "Well, then I guess we've got feed enough to run us. We won't have to send a wagon back after all. Oh, good evening again, Mr. Tasker! We thought you South Benders had us in a hole, but I guess we'll make out. Looks so, anyhow."

"You understand, Captain Frezzell," Tasker answered. "We jest natu'ally won't spare no time to let you put a wagon across tomorrow. An' the boat's laid up fer the night, so you're out."

"Yes, I know," Frezzell replied in great friendliness. "It's all right. That's all right. We got just a little hot under the collar for a minute back yonder, but no hard feelings, I hope. It looks now as if we'll not have any trouble about feed for the teams. Yep, yep, we'll make out fine tomorrow, I guess mebby, so it's all right, Mr. Tasker."

"I'll say it's all right! With us, every minute counts on this trip!" Tasker appeared to be looking for trouble. "Holdin' up fer one o' your wagons to cross might land us out at the gold fields jest a little mite late."

"Of course—of course." Frezzell turned to wave an arm toward the river. "Boys, you better get the cattle watered. Drive 'em downstream."

Tasker laughed. "Well, now that's nice of you!" he sneered, as the other South Bend men stood smiling. "Glad your crowd's so accommodatin'. Mighty good thing fer you, too! If you'd try to rile the water fer our mules, some o' our fellows might git a little testy."

"No use of getting into trouble when it can be avoided, Mr. Tasker," the captain answered smoothly. "Every train has to look out for its own interests the best way it can."

"No fight in this outfit!" Tasker laughed again. "Come on back, fellows."

"No, no fight. The meek inherit the earth you know, Mr. Tasker, if they're enterprising enough. And what they get, they hold onto. That's the one good quality we've got."

IV

COME OFF THAT BOAT

LONG after dark, three men set out stealthily from the ox train. They cut straight across the prairie to a good, safe distance from the South Bend wagons before they swung about toward the ferryman's house. Nearly all the members of the company that held the road to the river crossing had put their campfires out and rolled in for the night, but there was still a light at the ferryman's.

The ferryman was alone, and he was in a dour mood. Opening his door a few inches, he stood with his foot against it and glared out at the three visitors who had appeared so very quietly. He had taken off his shirt, his boots, and his socks. In his right hand he held a broad-bladed razor. His leather-like face had been scraped clean, but his neck was still covered with lather.

"We're from the Rock Island train that's lined up behind the mules," began the man standing in the light from the door crack. "I'm Captain Frezzell, and these two are Joe Barnett, our wagon master, and Gale Hedges. We want to come in and talk. Sorry to interrupt you, but it's important for us. You can go right along with your shaving, Mr. Sebastian."

"Well, that's all right," the ferryman answered genially. "It's all right just so you ain't lined up with that yalla-livered Tasker. Come on in." He drew his foot from the door and moved back in what proved to be the larger of two small rooms.

A table of rough oak stood against the wall, opposite a fire-place in which were a few dying embers. Near it were four strong chairs with wooden seats. On the table was a lighted candle. Beside the candle, a tiny mirror stood propped against a smoke-blackened stew-pan filled with hot water.

"You sound as if you don't like Tasker," Hedges ventured, as he and his two companions crossed the floor. "We don't like him, either. We've had words with him over wanting to send an empty wagon across your ferry to bring back feed for our cattle."

"I know about that!" was the answer. "Sit down. He's warned me what'll happen to me if I let your wagon go across. Go across my ferry, mind you!" He sat before the mirror, squinting into it. "I had words with 'im, but . . ." He scraped the razor noisily up one side of his neck, and talked only when he held the blade poised at the end of a stroke. "This razor could have a better edge, but—some of 'is friends drug 'im off where I couldn't reach 'im—or mebby we wouldn't 'ave stopped at words."

He swished the razor back and forth in the stew-pan to rinse off the lather, then resumed conversation. "I wish I could favor you. I'd take your—I'd take your whole train over ahead o' theirn if I could. But they've got a lawyer along, so Tasker says, an' I've—got a public ferry franchise here. Have to—take travelers over as—they come and—play no favors—or I'll lose the franchise."

"We didn't come to ask you to ferry us over, Mr. Sebastian,". Frezzell said. "We wondered if we couldn't buy your boat, since you'll have a new one up tomorrow. Buy it and let it drop down the river tonight to the old crossing."

"That pony girl, eh?" The ferryman chuckled. "I thought she had something on 'er mind the way she asked questions. She tell you, you can buy the boat?" He smiled at them as he got up, dipped one end of a grimy towel into the stew-pan, and scrubbed his face. "It was seein' that pony girl that set me thinkin' I was due for a clean-up. Eight days since the last girl passed, and eight days since I shaved. Did she prod you up to buy the boat?"

"Well," Frezzell admitted guardedly, "it was her idea."

"How much did she have it figgered you could likely buy it for?" he asked, as he began to make vigorous use of the dry end of the towel.

Frezzell and Barnett glanced at each other questioningly. "The joke of it is, she did suggest a price," the captain confessed. "She said forty or fifty dollars."

The ferryman scraped the razor noisily.

"Ferry tolls tomorrow and a little mite over, eh? Knows the mule train'll have to cross anyhow. I thought she was figgerin' that out. Well, I accommodate the ladies! Where's your fifty dollars?"

Frezzell could hardly keep still in his chair. "Here!" he exclaimed in unconcealed surprise. "Right here! Two twenties and a ten." The three coins clinked on the table. "And we have *two* lawyers in our party, so we had to bring along a bill of sale for you to sign."

"Here's ink, and a pen to sign with." Barnett placed an inkhorn and a pen on the table.

The ferryman sat down again. "You'll have a fight to hold that boat," he remarked, as if he were reconsidering.

"We'll take care of that end of it," Hedges assured him.

"Other party's twice as big as yourn. An' I'm not wishin' trouble on you. I warn you."

"We'll risk that." The captain pushed the paper across the table to him.

"Understand, I keep the cable an' the tackle. You'll have to pole 'er when you get 'er down below."

"That'll suit us tiptop!" The captain was extremely affable, but nervously eager to conclude the purchase. "Stream's good depth for poling though, is it?"

"Easy for poles. Good landing, too, both sides, with this high water." The ferryman signed his name laboriously. "Well, here's your bill o' sale. Hope there ain't no bad trouble in it."

"You keep the cable and the tackle," the captain said, "and, of course, you also keep quiet till tomorrow morning."

"Me?" The ferryman took out a deerskin pouch and dropped the gold pieces in, smiling all the while. "I wish you luck." Then he dried his razor and began to strop it.

"As you've no doubt noticed, Mr. . . ." Frezzell studied the paper. "Mr. Senter? S-E-N-T-E-R? Is that it?"

"Sintan," the ferryman said, "Sebastian Sintan."

"You've noticed, Mr. Sintan, that you're selling to Gale Hedges here, so that Barnett and I can legally sign as witnesses to your signature. There, Joe, put your name right under mine."

"Now," said Barnett, as he was signing, "we know who's going to cross this river first."

"Mebby you know—mebby you don't!" the ferryman answered.

"We'll cross first, or we'll know the reason why!" the wagon master exclaimed.

"You let the lines run through them pulleys a-tall when you cast off, an' mebby you won't be first to cross," Sintan warned. "The pulleys squeak so they wake the dead. An' that'd make the other fellows wonder what was up."

"We'll be careful," the captain assured him.

"I'll go tie the ropes so all you have to do is unhook an' drop the snatch blocks overboard. Think you can manage after that? And not get carried past the crossing down below?"

"I used to be captain of a steamboat," Frezzell informed him.

Sintan smiled and reached out a hand. "Then, Captain, I guess your train'll be the first across!"

"Well, we'll see. We'll just kind of see about that."

The ferryman stood chuckling, as he gave his razor a final stropping on the palm of his hand. The others bade him good night and very quietly departed.

Long before daylight, the ox teams were spanned in as noiselessly as possible. A few men of the mule train were up, but it was too dark for them to see whether the boat was gone or what was happening behind them. They listened in astonishment as the lumbering wagons were swung about and started rearward toward the road that led to the old crossing.

A little later some of the listeners went up the road to where the Rock Island train had been, to be sure their ears were not deceiving them.

"Too bad," one of them declared. "That louse Tasker ought to be thrown out! We ought not to stand for a jasper like him! Do you 'low they've quit? Or only gone to get feed?"

The ox train traveled about a mile before it came to the old road. When Brush's and Polly's wagons reached the river, the boat was drawn up at the bank, and a dozen men with rifles at hand were guarding it. Every man in the train had buckled on his belt, in which he carried a knife and a pistol.

"Don't they know yet what's happened to 'em up yonder?" one of the guards asked.

"Let them worry about that!" Barnett replied, as he promptly took charge of the work at the new ferry. "One wagon and two yoke of oxen only can go over at a load. Unhitch the extra pairs and get 'em right across so's they'll be nearer the hay. Don't waste any more time shaking hands with yourselves!

We're still on the wrong side of this river. It's daylight now, and we've got no time to lose."

An empty wagon drawn by a single pair of red steers turned out of the road well back in the line, and moved in ahead of Brush to be first aboard and bring back the feed.

The loading took very little time, but the old low flatboat was heavy. The men poled it slowly to the far bank and then poled it slowly back. There was a good strip of timber on each side of the stream, chiefly oak, but with a few hickories and butternuts, and here and there a clump of willows at the water's edge.

The woods hid the train, as well as the men at work, from everyone at the other crossing place about a mile up the river.

"Even if they can't see us," Frezzell said, "they can hear the clatter of the hoofs and when the wagons go on and off the boat. We've got to be ready for a mighty mad lot of South Benders around here any minute. Zenas, string about eight men with rifles along back to guard the train. They're to help the drivers fight off attack, and they're to stay with the wagons no matter what happens. You come here again as soon as they're set."

The crossing proceeded without interruption until nearly nine, when twenty or more men from the mule train came down along the river bank. Gale Hedges was the first to see them. "Here they come at last!" he called, when there was a moment of quiet.

Tasker, who was in the lead, grew purple with rage when he saw what was happening. "Come off that boat!" he yelled.

"You think we'll let you steal a public ferry and hold our train up? Then that's where you miss count! Come on, fellows, take it!"

"Easy, Tasker!" Frezzell warned. "Slow up! And slow up fast! We meek folks hold what we get! And we warned you last night! Those rifles are loaded, and they're pointing in your direction, you'll notice. Keep off, Tasker, the boat belongs to one of our men."

"Who said it does!"

"His property, bought and paid for. Yes, sir. And he's asked for our aid and protection. We're giving him both. We've got a legal right to shoot the gizzards out of you if you try to take it. And we mean to do just that."

"Sebastian don't say you own it!" Tasker answered.

"Mr. Sintan can say what he likes, of course, but that don't make any difference to us," returned the captain.

"Might let him look at the bill of sale," suggested Hedges, who was on the boat.

"Stop right there!" Zenas Rose interrupted, as Tasker started forward. Zenas had drawn his Colt revolving pistol. "Tasker, you don't go on this boat, no matter what. And don't come any closer, either. Here, Gale, hand that paper out to me cautious, and let me show it to him."

Rose reached out from the bank, brought the bill of sale around, and held it in front of the South Bend man, the muzzle of the pistol a few inches from it.

"No need to cover 'im with a shootin' iron, Mister," one of the other men of the mule train remarked. "We're not making any threats with firearms."

"We don't intend to let this man Tasker grab the boat, or the bill of sale either!" Rose answered. "We mean to hang onto the two of 'em!"

"May I look at that?" one of the South Bend men asked. "My name is Husted Butler."

When the captain nodded assent, Butler stepped up. Without hesitation, he shouldered Tasker, who was the larger, aside, and read the document carefully. "Thank you!" he said and rejoined his own group. The men gathered about him, talking in low tones.

"That piece o' paper won't stop me gettin' back that boat!" Tasker declared.

"Tasker," Butler said, "you're talking too much."

"Drive your team on, Freddie!" Joe Barnett ordered. "You're holding up the line. You can see just as good from the other side of the river."

A wagon was driven noisily onto the boat, and the polers took it to the other bank while Tasker's party was still in whispered conference. Polly Kent came back on the return trip. She led her saddled mare off and then went up to Captain Frezzell.

"Sebastian Sintan, the ferryman, shouted across to me a little while ago," she whispered so that no one else could hear. "He told me he'd seen the sheriff ride up. He'll have to tell the sheriff, he says, that he's sold the boat, or else he'll get into trouble. He told me the sheriff will come right down here, and he also told me to warn you you'd better be careful."

5

Frezzell laughed. "Good old Sebastian! Or did he only holler so's you'd see what a handsome young lad he is when his eight-day beard's off?"

Another wagon rolled onto the boat.

"Barnett! Here a minute!" the captain shouted when he could make himself heard. But he lowered his voice as the wagon master came close. "Joe, Sintan's sent word the sheriff's happened along, and may drop in on us. Pass the word, but let's keep it quiet from the other crowd if we can."

"Well, what if he does come?" Barnett asked. "What difference does that make to us?"

"In that case, warn the boys to keep the ferry over against the other bank as long as he stays around. I mean if he starts making things hot."

"Hey, Hedges, wait!" Barnett shouted.

"Joe," the captain said, "you take Gale's place. We may need him here."

The wagon master jumped aboard the boat, which had been stopped a few feet from the landing, and spoke to Hedges, who handed over the pole he had been using. Then he leaped to the bank.

"We've got to be ready for a visit from the sheriff," the captain told him.

"He's coming now," Polly whispered. "Anyway, there's someone coming with the ferryman, and both of them are mounted."

A tall, tanned, and grizzled man in a crumpled gray hat and a mud-splattered corduroy suit rode down past the wagons on a lean bay mare. Her belly and legs were coated with mud which was beginning to dry. The mare stopped beside Polly Kent and nudged her to invite attention. The tall man looked the two belligerent groups over placidly. Sintan, following on a clean little white pony, drew rein a little behind his companion, and gave Captain Frezzell a quick glance of warning.

"Which of you is Gale Hedges?" the stranger inquired.

"I am," Hedges answered.

"Sebastian here tells me he's sold you his ferry. I have county business on beyond and will have to go across."

"We'll take you over," Hedges replied, "as soon as the boat comes back from the other side."

The man on the bay mare produced some coins, selecting two. "Here's the toll." He held out the money.

"There'll be no charge," Hedges answered. "This is not a public ferry. We didn't buy the ferry franchise. This just happens to be a boat I own. I'm letting my friends use it, and so I'll let you."

"Must have a lawyer in your party, too." The newcomer smiled as he dropped the coins back into his pocket. "Sebastian, where's the public ferry you're supposed to be running here?"

"As I told you before, Sheriff, the new boat's due up any time now," the ferryman answered.

"You the sheriff?" Tasker shouted. "Didn't he call you sheriff?"

"Sounded so. Yes, I'm John Cole, sheriff."

"All right!" Tasker came striding toward him. "We demand you to put this ferry back—and now! Back up yonder where it come from! This man says he's bought it! But that trick don't work on us, Sheriff! That don't leave him run this boat down here off'n the main road in the middle o' the night, and hold us travelers up from crossin'! Us that come to the landin' first! Not fer a minute it don't!"

"Have you a bill of sale, Hedges?" the sheriff asked.

Gale handed the bill up to him, and the sheriff read it carefully.

"Looks legal enough," he commented, as he handed it back.

"Am I right?" Tasker cried. "Paper or no paper, can he do that?"

"Come right down to it," the sheriff answered, "I suppose you've raised a point that only a judge can decide."

"Then I demand action! I demand the arrest of this whole crowd!"

"That's a crazy play, Tasker!" the South Bend man named Butler interposed, as he came forward. "Sheriff, how long can a ferryman hold his franchise here after he sells the only boat he has in operation and stops giving the public any service?" he asked.

"You're the South Bend lawyer, eh?" the sheriff said. "Well, Sebastian, that's a question for you to think about."

"I'll give 'em service as soon as the new boat comes," the ferryman answered uneasily.

"How do we know it will ever come?" Butler asked. "How do we know there is a new boat as he says? I'd say you've already lost your franchise, Sintan, if we care to press the matter."

"Hedges," the sheriff said, "that boat of yours across the river is tied up. How long is it going to stay there?"

"As long as this crowd stands around making threats to seize possession of it!" Frezzell interrupted. "If they clear out of here, we'll take you across. And we'll sell the boat back to Sintan if he wants it, just as soon as we put the river there behind us."

"How much?" Sintan asked anxiously.

"Well, Gale, it's your boat," the captain remarked with a broad smile.

"Oh, say thirty or forty cents," Hedges answered. "It won't be worth that much to me, once we all get across. But we know when we hold the whip hand, and I won't shade the price."

"Fair enough, Sebastian," the sheriff said.

"Fair nothin'!" Tasker cried. "That's a trick! Nothin' but! A dirty trick to wedge in ahead of us! I demand this man Frezzell's arrest! An' Hedges!"

"I've no time to waste here making arrests," replied the sheriff. "It just happens I've important business for the county on the other side."

"Stop it, Tasker!" Butler warned. "Arrest them for what? What charge can you make that will hold?"

"Butler, you keep out!" Tasker shot back at him. "I'm doin' this with the captain's backin'!"

"Where is the captain of your train?" the sheriff inquired.

"Laid up in 'is wagon," Tasker replied. "Bad hurt where a mule kicked 'im."

"The longer you delay things here, the longer we'll be getting across," Butler protested.

"You keep out! I'm playin' this hand!" Tasker turned to Cole. "I demand the arrest of all these men standin' right here!" He pointed to Frezzell, Zenas Rose, Hedges, and two others who were near them.

In a very leisurely way, Sheriff Cole dismounted. "If you say *demand*—and speak with the authority of your captain— why, there's only one thing for me to do, of course," he said. "Captain Frezzell, you and your men had better come along peaceably with me."

"How long is this going to take, Sheriff?" Frezzell asked, more than a little anxiously.

"Well," the sheriff answered, "for your men who will have to fight the case, oh, not more than four, five days."

"Four or five days!" several exclaimed aghast. The men all gazed in consternation at the captain.

Tasker was grinning.

"Tasker, stop it, I tell you!" Butler warned. "You're getting us all into a hole!"

Cole turned so that his back was toward the South Bend men, who were only a few steps away. He looked at Frezzell, and said in a low voice, "Come on, play the hand out with this fool. Maybe we can all get across before night." Aloud he said, "How about it, Frezzell? Coming peaceably or not?"

"Why, of course, we'll go peaceably."

"All right!" Cole snapped out. "Tasker, you round up seven or eight men as witnesses for your side and bring them along!"

"Look here, Tasker," Butler exclaimed, "we won't stand for any seven or eight men being delayed here four or five days! And have the whole train held up indefinitely besides!"

"Come on!" the sheriff broke in. "I've no time to waste!"

"Sheriff, wait a minute!" Tasker called. "Who's the man that thunk up this slick-alec trick of buyin' the boat? You give me a chance to lick 'im, an' have it fixed so's the side that wins the fight gits the boat, an' I'll call the arrests off. Won't be no delay about that!"

The Rock Island men looked at Polly and began to grin.

"I'll lick the man that sprung that, so help me!" Tasker hitched up his belt. "I'll lick 'im, or I'll go through with these arrests, if not a one here ever gits to California!"

Polly, who had been an interested listener, became embarrassed by the sudden switching of attention to herself.

Sebastian Sintan let out a guffaw. "Pony girl," he exclaimed, "my money's on you! Tasker, given somebody was around to see fair play, you couldn't even lick a woman! Not this pony girl, nohow!"

"Was it her idea?" Sheriff Cole inquired.

"She was the one that suggested it," Frezzell answered.

Cole chuckled as he said, "Tasker, I'll give you a couple of minutes to round up the men that want to stay over for the trial. If nobody wants to stay, I'll pick out seven or eight myself and hold them as material witnesses."

"Sheriff," Butler interrupted, "this man has no authority from the members of this train."

"My authority comes from the captain."

"I don't believe that," Butler answered.

"Butler," Tasker snarled threateningly, "you watch your talk!"

"I don't believe this man has any authority," Butler repeated.

"Come, Frezzell," Cole said. "You South Bend men come along, too. I won't have any fight start here between your two parties while I'm gone. And I mean to see that the Rock Island boys keep the boat till this case is tried and settled." With that he and the men whose arrest Tasker had demanded started up the road.

"And some of you go up and tell the captain what kind of fix this fool Tasker has got us into," Butler suggested.

"You can't talk that way about me!" Tasker blustered, "not for a minute!"

"I am talking that way about you!" This time Butler spoke very quietly.

"All right! Make good on it!"

"Here, no shooting!" a South Bend man shouted.

The two who stood facing each other started to draw their pistols, but one of the others snatched Tasker's weapon away before he could reach it. Butler, who was much the quicker, had already covered his man, and could have shot him down before he was disarmed. Butler now returned his weapon to its holster.

"You give me back my gun, Honus!" Tasker demanded. "Or you grab his'n, too!"

"He was set to bore you, you fool, if he'd wanted to!" The man who had snatched the pistol kept it. He was a brisk, hard

chap under thirty, and wore a Mexican army hat with a
bullet hole through its crown. "The Lieutenant's too all-fired
quick for you," he said now. "Long as I keep your gun, there
won't be nobody shovelin' down sod on top of you. And we
won't be held up here for a murder trial."

"Come on, South Bend!" the sheriff called from up the road.

"Bring Tasker with us, Honus!" Butler rapped out.

Polly noticed that Butler spoke this time in the tone of one
used to giving commands and to having them obeyed. She
looked at him with suddenly quickened interest. He was
young, black-haired, olive-complexioned, quietly observant,
and swift of movement. He impressed the girl as being cautious
but withal determined and resourceful. The ready acceptance
of his leadership by the men of the South Bend train alarmed
her. He seemed so controlled and now so sure of himself that
she wished he were on her side in this trouble instead of on the
other.

"From now on, we'll keep Tasker in his place," he said.
"And we'll find out just what that place is! Take charge,
Honus, while I talk to the sheriff. And clear all our men away
from here."

The man in the army hat saluted in military fashion, and
Butler hurried off. Tasker without a pistol was much less
belligerent, but Polly could still hear some threatening talk
from him as he and the others left the river.

"Boys, you keep the wagons going over!" Frezzell shouted,
"And we'll fight this out! By the jumpin' Jupiter, we'll
fight it!"

V

TASTE IT, MR. ROSE

THERE was no fighting at the ferry, and Polly did not see
Tasker there again. The sheriff kept the South Bend men
away until after three in the afternoon, when word was sent to
him that the bill of sale had been torn up and that Sintan
could have his boat.

More than an hour later, the wagons and the oxen were still in
the woods west of the old crossing place, just as they had been
left in the hurry of getting them off the ferry and out of the
way. Polly's wagon was farthest from the river, and Frezzell
and a few men of the train had gathered about it.

"Come here a minute, Brush!" Zenas Rose shouted, "you
and your wife! Your daughter, too!"

"They've been acting as if there's some kind of trouble
again," Ann said anxiously.

"We'll go see." Brush emptied the washbasin he had been using. "Come along with us, Daughter." He reached for the towel which his wife was holding out to him and started up the road, drying his hands and face as he went.

"Where's the Kent girl?" the captain asked.

"She's not here right now, Captain Frezzell," Eusebia answered. "When the men got the train across and were able to look after the oxen she'd been guarding for 'em, she rode on a ways with the sheriff."

"Ever been in her wagon, any of you?" Frezzell asked abruptly.

The mother and the daughter, startled by his tone, looked at each other questioningly.

"I never have," Ann told him.

"Neither have I," Mrs. Brush said.

"Nor I," added her husband.

"Just climb up and look in, one of you."

Brush climbed to the seat and looked into the wagon. In a moment he eased himself to the ground. His eyes were wide with astonishment, but he did not say anything.

"What is it?" Eusebia asked anxiously.

"Whisky kegs," her husband answered.

"Kegs of whisky!" Zenas Rose corrected.

"Whisky!" Ann repeated, horrified.

"A whole wagonload of it," Rose stated.

"I don't believe it!" Ann exclaimed.

"Well, I can't believe it either," her mother said, but not with the girl's confidence.

"Nine kegs of whisky! Nine!" Rose repeated.

"Mercy me!" Mrs. Brush stared at the wagon, but she did not go near it.

"It's not whisky!" Ann declared. "It can't be!"

"We uncovered all nine kegs," Frezzell told the astonished Brushes. "To keep 'em from rolling around, she's got 'em lashed with tarred ropes run through eyebolts in the floor and sides of the wagon box."

"I don't believe it!" Ann was fighting back her tears.

"Hush, dear!" Her mother put an arm about her.

"She's smart!" Rose said. "We've just had one sample of how smart she is on this ferryboat dicker, but—by crackey! Why, at the mines, the liquor she's got in those kegs would be worth Lord knows how much—it's weight in gold!"

"The point is," Captain Frezzell interposed, "we thought you and your wife, and your young daughter here, ought to know about this before going any farther with her. It beats me! I can't figger any decent woman of any age, let alone a young girl, starting out by herself on a two thousand mile journey like this with a lot of hard liquor aboard."

"Well," Brush commented, "can you figure *any* woman doing that? I can't. But how do you know it's whisky?"

"Word come up from Terry Hut about this lady," Rose answered.

"Know anything about her?" the captain asked. "Who and what she really is?"

"Yes!" Ann spoke defiantly. "She's good plum through!"

"We know only what she's told us," Brush answered.

"And I'm betting she's not told you much!" Rose cut in again. "Hasn't done much talking about herself, has she?"

"She hasn't had time to talk! She's been busy every minute!" Ann reminded them. "She's been helping you folks, too!"

"Smart, yes," the captain agreed. "Smart, tight-mouthed, and hard as nails in a pinch, I'd say, but she didn't look to me like *that* kind."

"Still, there's the whisky!" Rose laughed. "Where's Hedges? Him and me had one argument about Miss Terry Hut back in Rock Island. Maybe he'd like to speak up for her now."

"He's helping pole Sintan's boat back up the river," Frezzell answered. "But here comes the girl herself. Our boys aren't many of them heavy drinkers, Brush, but we don't intend to have any wagonload of redeye trailing along handy to tempt 'em! I can tell you that!"

The girl came riding through the woods in the winding road and drew up her pony beside them. "The sheriff told me of a creek we can reach before night if we start soon enough, Mr. Brush," she said, noticing how strangely they were all watching her. She looked at them inquiringly. "He thinks we'll have rain and a heavy road tomorrow. And if we stay here tonight, we'll have to cover twenty miles without a stop to reach Washington, or we'll run out of feed for the teams. He says there's not a house nor a turned furrow of sod in the whole twenty miles."

As she talked, she looked at Brush and waited, but he did not speak.

"They say you have whisky in your wagon!" Ann suddenly spoke up.

The girl on the pony merely glanced at the younger girl and then turned to the men. "Do they?" she asked quietly. "Who's been messing in my wagon?"

"Miss Kent, we heard about your load of liquor, so we looked to see." Frezzell spoke reluctantly.

"What business is it of yours, Captain, what I have in my wagon?" she asked. "I'm not traveling with your train!"

"We don't intend to have the stuff anywhere around to tempt our men!" Rose answered.

"The road's free, Mr. Rose!" Polly answered, "as you yourself were kind enough to tell me back in Rock Island." Dismounting, she took her rifle from the saddle, climbed up her wagon, and hung the gun in its loops inside the wagon cover. "Who did that?" she demanded. "Who mussed up my wagon like this?"

"Nobody touched your whisky, if that's what's troubling you," Rose answered. "It's all there, Miss. Be worth a lot of money time you land it out in California. And I guess it ought to carry safe all the way. You got the kegs roped down so they can't bump around and spring a leak, I notice. Mighty smart lady."

"Who's been in my wagon?" the girl insisted. "You?"

"I looked in. Moved things around some, too. Yes, I looked in the wagon some." Rose laughed.

Polly still leaned under the hood, staring in. She jerked out an old buffalo robe, and, after it, a blue blanket which she began to fold.

"I don't call this funny, Mr. Rose!" she said, turning to face him. "You heard about my load of liquor, did you, Captain Frezzell! Who told you about it?"

"When a lady heading west loads up with a cargo of redeye, word of it gets around quite some," Rose interrupted. "Week ago, up at South Bend, some Terry Hut chap was telling on you. How you got a cooper shop boss down the Wabash to make you up a wagonload of whisky kegs for the trip to California."

"Oh, you got it from one of the South Bend men?"

"That's how, Miss," Frezzell answered.

"Who from?"

"All of 'em!" Rose was enjoying himself. "Guess we heard 'em all talk about it. You'd ought 'ave heard some that was said. Told us you was the lady, so we come to see."

At that moment Polly happened to glance at the side of her wagon cover where some large black lettering showed through. She stared at the splotch for a moment, then got down quickly and went around to look at the outside of the cover.

"Who painted 'Miss Terry Hut' on my wagon?" she demanded angrily.

Captain Frezzell and all the others, with the exception of Lester Lee and Freddie Dascomb, moved around beside her.

"Well, tarnation!" the captain exclaimed. "Who did that?" He stepped up and touched a finger to a letter. "It's still wet. Just been painted."

Rose laughed.

"Did you do that?" the girl asked him.

"There's once you guessed wrong," he answered.

Polly looked at him steadily for a moment, then at the two who were still standing apart from the others. She walked around the wagon tongue, took off her coat and laid it on the seat. Then she stepped over beside young Lee and grasped him by the wrist.

"There's fresh black paint on Lester Lee's hands!" she announced. "You painted my wagon cover! Painted 'Miss Terry Hut' on it! First, you men pass the word that a lone girl from Terre Haute has a load of whisky! Then you label my wagon so that everyone who sees it will treat it as if it were a saloon! Do you think I'll let you give me such a reputation as that?"

Lester pulled away from her and picked up a can of black paint from behind a tree. "Aw, we didn't know about the whisky when we put the sign on," he grumbled. "Here, I'll paint the name out if you don't like it. But nearly every wagon's got something on it—nearly every wagon starting west, Miss Kent. Honest, we thought you'd want yours to have a name like the others."

"We!" Polly repeated. "So you didn't paint it because of the whisky!" She looked at Freddie Dascomb. "You helped, didn't you?"

Lester looked at Freddie, and both grinned. Lester made a sweep with the brush.

"Don't blacken it all out," Polly cried. "That would ruin the looks of the cover." The girl studied the lettering. "I don't like the 'Miss.' Paint that out and leave 'Terry Hut.' Now put a square blotch after it, like the one you've painted over the 'Miss,' to balance the name that's left."

"Lester, you picked a poor time for your fool prank!" Frezzell said frowningly.

"Prank!" Polly exclaimed. "You call this a prank?"

"By crackey!" Rose bent over and smacked his palm against his knee. "You'll have your trouble with that load of whisky before you go many miles farther!"

"Lester Lee," Polly said, "the least you can do for me now is to climb up, you and Freddie Dascomb, and get me out one of my kegs. I mean it! Since you men have been told so much, maybe I haven't any whisky left! Get me out a keg. Any one of the nine; it doesn't make any difference which."

"We don't want any of that stuff opened here!" Frezzell shouted.

"I'm going to find out all about this!" Polly answered.

"Climb up!" Lester urged, low voiced, and the two got to the seat and went to work.

"Just roll back the things on top," Polly directed. "They'll roll now that I've straightened them. They didn't have to be mussed up, Mr. Rose. Reach down, Freddie, and untie the rope, don't cut it."

"Uh!" Lester grunted. "Here she comes! Hist it! Now rest it on the seat."

"Hold it there!" Polly ordered, getting up beside the two men. Fishing out a hammer, she pounded the bung, first on one side and then on the other, until it loosened and she could pull it out. "Now roll the keg so it will pour, but don't let it spill."

The boys rolled it carefully, and Polly held a tin cup under the bunghole. Suddenly both boys burst out laughing.

"What is it?" Captain Frezzell asked.

Polly climbed down and held out the cup in front of Zenas Rose. "Taste it!" she urged. "Taste it, Mr. Rose! You look like a mighty good judge of whisky!"

"What is it?" Frezzell asked again.

"Parched hominy corn!" Polly told him. "A keg made to keep whisky in will keep water out when I'm getting my wagon across rivers out West, where there aren't any ferries. I have nine kegs of parched hominy corn, Mr. Rose! New kegs in which the corn will keep sweet. Mrs. Brush, I spent most of the winter parching corn and packing it into the kegs to keep dry."

"There! I told you!" Mrs. Brush cried joyously.

"And Mr. Rose," Polly went on, "I roped the kegs fast so they'd keep the wagon afloat going across the rivers when we come to them. Hammer the bung in tight, will you, boys? I may need every grain of that corn, and I want it crisp, not moldy."

The boys had accidentally knocked her coat down on the ground, so she picked it up before continuing. "Tie the keg back where it belongs. Besides the corn, I have bedding, clothes to last two years, a medicine chest, a caddy of tea, a coffeepot and green coffee, a three-gallon camp kettle, also one that holds three quarts, a couple of frying pans, a big and a little stew-pan, knives, forks, spoons, three tin dippers, and my old doll with a battered head made of leather. Now that you know everything there is in my wagon, you'll never have an excuse to come messing in it again, Mr. Rose."

"Polly, I don't blame you for being mad!" Eusebia cried. "We knew you didn't have whisky—Colin and Ann and I—didn't we?"

"No," Frezzell said, "they stuck mighty loyal to you. I'm sorry, Miss Kent, sorry about the whole business."

"Me, too!" Lester, still in the wagon, grinned impishly.

"Mr. Rose, no man from Terre Haute ever said I had whisky. They know better than that down there. If apologizing comes so hard, maybe you can tell me who spread that lie."

"The South Benders." Rose laughed to hide his discomfiture. "Parched corn, eh? That's a wagonload to cross the plains with!"

Polly unsaddled Keiëta, and when she began to hitch her team, Brush laughed heartily. He flipped the towel at Rose good-naturedly and put his arm about Ann.

"Why, even a man could live a mighty long time on good parched hominy corn," he remarked.

"Don't go off angry, Miss Kent!" Frezzell urged. "You stay here, and welcome. We apologize. We all apologize!"

"I'm going on tonight to where Sheriff Cole said there's a creek and a place to camp."

"So are we!" Ann said. "Father, let's hitch up!"

"We'll be right with you, Polly!" Brush called, as he hurried away. "Right with you!"

"But I want to know who spread that story about me!" The girl's indignation had not cooled. "That's something I mean to find out!"

"Ask this chap Butler, that's coming," Frezzell suggested. "Butler," he called, "somebody in your crowd started a story about this girl freighting whisky to the mines."

"Yes, I heard it," Butler answered, looking at Polly with a wrinkling of the brows.

"Well, she's got nine full kegs of parched hominy corn. Nine kegs full. Just showed it to us."

Butler's brows cleared suddenly, and he smiled at the girl.

"Who started that story?" Polly asked him, noticing his grave smile as she talked to him.

"Tasker," Butler answered, and stood looking at her. "I came over to ask if you'd missed anything, Miss Kent. Some of our boys saw Tasker climb into your wagon while it was standing off alone beside the road yesterday afternoon just before your train drew up. We know he's a liar, and he may be a thief as well."

"Oh!" Polly cried. "That explains it! He climbed in my wagon and saw the kegs there. That's why he asked me last evening if I wanted to trade loads with him. I thought he meant the sacks of corn I had on a pony."

"He said he looked in the wagon because a Terre Haute man had told him a girl with ponies had started north with a load of whisky, and that you were the girl."

"He's a good fast liar, that fellow!" Frezzell exclaimed.

"We're getting rid of him," Butler stated. "In the first place he's not a South Bend man, and we'd like to have you know that. Our men will push him on across the river when they get the ferry back in place. He may be on this side already.

If he stole anything from you, we'll overtake him. I don't think he did, though, Miss Kent, because our boys were watching him."

"I've no way of knowing now whether anything was taken or not," Polly said. "Mr. Rose here messed things so in my wagon it would take me half an hour to find out, and I haven't time. Thank you, Mr. Butler! I don't think I've lost anything."

"Tonight you and Brush better camp here near us," Frezzell urged. "We've got so many oxen galled and petered out that we can't risk moving on till morning. And since Tasker thinks you've got whisky, he may raid you if he runs across you out yonder alone."

"I just wish he'd try it!" Polly answered, then turning, she called, "are you ready, Mr. Brush?"

"Strike ahead!" Brush shouted. "We're just about set to tag along."

VI

PLEASE DON'T FIGHT

THE oxen of the Rock Island train were fed the last of the hay and corn next morning, and all day they plodded across an unsettled prairie in a pouring rain against a beating head wind. The road was soft, and in places the last of the wagons sank to their axles in the mud.

All through the late afternoon the cattle had to be prodded constantly. Just before dark they arrived at a farm near Washington, in Washington County, some twenty miles from Sintan's ferry, where there was plenty of feed. The men had walked all the way to save their teams and were cold, wet, and exhausted.

They learned that a six-mule team with a man of Tasker's description driving, had passed a few hours earlier, and that a short time later, Brush and the girl with the ponies had stopped to load on all the corn and hay they could haul.

Next day, the ox train arrived at a place called Fairplay, twelve miles south, in time to cross the Skunk River by ferry before camping. Another day's travel of twelve miles took the train to Fairfield, in Jefferson County. Here it again turned west, heading this time for the ferry at Ottumwa, which was to be the next camping place, twenty miles away on the Des Moines River.

During this brief time, Polly and the Brushes camped miles ahead each night, but before taking to the road, they waited every morning until they could see the ox train approaching. Brush could not afford to lose touch with the Rock Islanders on the way to St. Joseph, where Doctor Brackett would be waiting with supplies. All the while, other wagon trains bound for El Dorado were swinging out of the byways into the road that led to the river crossings where there were ferries. It was this road that the Rock Island men were traveling.

Soon neither Brush nor Polly could distinguish one train from another at any distance, and at last they waited for Frezzell's party. Every night they camped near it, though they still tried to keep ahead.

For two weeks they had fine weather, the roads were at their best, and there was plenty of feed. They followed a long, dividing ridge through Monroe, Lucas, and Clarke counties, traveling nearly due west about twenty miles a day, then veered to the southwest through Ringgold County, and, after fording the Grand River, followed down the west bank into Missouri.

Throughout this region Polly saw with interest that there was a farm at every creek and wide stretches of unsettled country between the streams. But the travelers had no trouble getting feed for their cattle, and hay and corn were cheap. During this time, the animals all rounded out into good condition, and May and Kate, the two cows hitched with Colin's oxen, between them gave a full bucket of milk a day. Deer, prairie chicken, and quail were plentiful, and the old cock turkeys wakened the campers in the mornings with their gobbling.

On the twenty-eighth of April, after twenty-four days of travel, the Rock Island train ascended a hill that overlooked St. Joseph. During the last dozen miles it had passed numberless white-hooded prairie schooners camped by the roadside and a few that were moving slowly. Always the roads ahead were full of them.

From ridge crossings and hilltops, the Rock Island men had seen lines of emigrant wagons like their own heading toward the town on other roads. But they, as well as the men in the trains behind them, were still unaware of the vast proportions of this most amazing of migrations. They knew they had reached the Missouri River, the borderline of the peopled world. The sun was shining, spring had come, and they were confident. In their eagerness to cross and to hasten on along the unknown trail that led to the land of gold, they came, prodding their oxen and singing lustily:

"Oh, Susannah! Don't you cry for me!
I'm off to California with my washbowl on my knee!"

Brush was waiting on the hill. Both his wagon and Polly's were at the side of the road, the cattle and the two ponies in harness were unhitched and feeding. Brush seemed to be disheartened and bewildered. "May as well stop here!" he called to Joe Barnett, who was walking ahead of his train.

"No stop this side the river!" Joe shouted back.

"No need to hurry now," Colin answered. "Come over here."

Barnett swung out of the road. "Where's Captain Frezzell?" he asked. "He started ahead at daylight with Dimmock to look things over."

"Haven't seen anybody," Brush answered, as the two moved nearer to the brow of the hill.

"Well, what do you hear?" Barnett asked gaily.

"Hear?" Brush glanced at him in surprise. "It sounds to me like ten thousand mules braying yonder. Take a look at the jam down in St. Joe!"

Startled by the other's tone, the wagon master jerked his head around. "Will it mean a delay at the ferry?" he asked in sudden concern.

"What else can it mean?" Brush asked in return. "But there's Polly coming!" He took off his hat and held it up to attract her attention. "She'll be here in a minute. She rode down two or three hours ago to find out what the chances are. Better wait and see."

"Gee-rusalem! I can see for myself *now*!" Barnett exclaimed as he stared down the hill. "Nothing anywhere about the town but wagons, oxen, and mules! Gosh all fishhooks! Do you hear 'em bray? Boys!" He raised a hand as a signal for the train to halt. "Swing out o' the road awhile. And just look down there! You won't need to listen!"

The singing had ceased, except for a few voices back in the line. And now that the teams had stopped, the men could all hear the chorus of the mules.

"But that ain't 'Susannah' they're singing," someone shouted. And there was a moment of laughter as the men came hurrying to see.

"Well, Polly, how does it look?" Brush asked, as the girl rode up to them.

"It *couldn't* look worse," she told him. "It just couldn't possibly!"

"Good morning, Miss Kent!" Joe Barnett called. "I hardly knew you without that green coat of yours."

"Green! It's blue!" she replied as she nodded in greeting to several of the men who spoke to her. "Everything looks pretty blue just now. Captain Frezzell wants the train to wait here for him. He said to tell you he left Dimmock up here with his wagon."

"Some of you boys hunt around for Dimmock." Barnett turned and spoke to Polly again. "How soon do you think we can cross the Missouri?"

She answered wearily, "There's only one little ferry here at St. Joe, Mr. Barnett—a flatboat worked by two oars." The men drew close about her to listen. "Fifty wagons and their teams are all it can take across the river in a day. In a day and a night it can take seventy-five. And there are more than five thousand wagons now waiting ahead of us down there!"

"Five thousand!" a dozen men repeated in an outburst of consternation.

"Nobody ever dreamed there would be such a pouring in of people headed for the gold fields," Polly continued. "Not the least preparation has been made for them, nor for thirty thousand or more oxen and mules that are crowded in there."

"Then only the ones that pay high will cross!" Rose said. "We'll pay! We've got to get on!"

"We'll buy the ferry like we bought Sebastian's," Lester Lee put in.

"No, you'll not!" Polly answered. "You'll not buy this one. There are thousands of people watching that ferry all the time. And you'll not cross the river on it ahead of them, no matter how much you pay."

"Is the town as crowded as it looks?" Hedges asked.

"The streets are blocked solid with wagons lined up four abreast," Polly told him. "The teams have been unhitched and taken off to a place where there's room to feed them, but the wagons have been left there, every one with its tongue run under the body of the wagon ahead."

Many of the men, some from trains still plodding past, were now crowding around, grim, weary, and alarmed. From Polly they caught their first intimation of what the congestion in the town meant to them.

"That's the way it is," she said, "four wagons abreast, in the street alongside the river, and in the next one up, in the main street, which runs down to the ferry, and in two other cross streets."

"Gee-rusalem!" Barnett screwed up his face as if in sudden pain.

"Only a person walking or on a saddle horse can get past them," Polly went on. "And down close along the river are hundreds of yoked oxen or harnessed teams, their drivers waiting to hitch to when their turns come."

"Speak up a little, lady. We can't hear you!" came in a quavering request from the outer fringe of listeners.

Polly spoke louder this time. "One man told me he'd been waiting down there two days and nights. It would be a week, he thought, before the wagons locked in ahead of his would be out of the way. But he daren't lose his turn."

A stranger standing near by listening while he looked down at the animals and men below, said in measured tones, with the solemnity of a preacher, "This great tidal wave of humanity that is rolling from sea to sea cannot be held from sweeping on either by rivers, by prairies, or by mountains."

"You mean we can cross?" Barnett asked him. "How?" But as the stranger stood silently, the wagon master turned again to Polly.

"Out of our turn we can't!" she said. "If anybody *could* get a wagon through to that ferry out of turn, he'd be shot down the minute he tried it. But no one can. The people—they're desperate! Thousands of them! Some seem beside themselves —stunned! They've staked everything they have in the world on getting to California before snow and ice block the mountain passes."

"They're no worse off than we are," a Rock Islander named Hill said. "A lot of us in this train have staked every blessed thing we have."

"Five thousand wagons crossing, seventy-five in a day, would be . . ." Wagon master Barnett looked about helplessly from man to man. "Somebody tell me how long that would take."

"Two months," Polly answered.

"Two months!" several cried in chorus.

"And more wagons are coming, coming by the hundreds and hundreds every day," the girl added.

"Two months!" And Zenas Rose reached out and caught Barnett by a shoulder. "Listen!" he shouted. "We've got to be halfway to California in two months! Got to be! All right, turn right straight around now and head north up the river for Weston! We can't drive across this danged Missouri! We've got to have a ferry! There's one up at Weston!"

"Turn north with empty wagons?" Gale Hedges asked.

"Oh, we'll take on supplies before we start," Rose answered.

"Mr. Rose," Polly said, "every state in the Union is sending wagon trains, has been sending them, to the only four points on this river where there are ferries. The captain of a steamboat told me that Council Bluffs, Weston, and Fort Leavenworth are just as crowded as St. Joe is. At Fort Leavenworth, he said, there are two ferries, but more wagon trains are waiting there. He said that . . ."

"Stop a minute! I want to ask something!" Barnett interrupted. "Do you know if Frezzell's seen anything of Doctor Brackett and our supplies? They should've been up by steamboat."

"He hadn't heard when I started back from town," Polly answered. "But it's hard to find anything. The warehouses are filled, so all the boats from St. Louis are unloading their freight right on the river bank and leaving it there unprotected from thieves or the weather."

'Then some of us have got to get down there in jig time and look after things!" Barnett declared.

"Well, *you* don't have to wait for supplies, Miss!" Rose glowered at the girl. "Why don't you float across this river on your whisky kegs, like you're going to float across the other rivers, and strike on west without holding up for anybody?"

"With my ponies, Mr. Rose," Polly answered, "I can wait here three weeks after your oxen have crossed and still reach California before you."

"Says you!"

"Hanged if I don't believe it, too!" Barnett exclaimed. "Come on, boys, prod 'em along! We'll get down close as we can to where the boats are unloading."

"Captain Frezzell said you were not to take the train down there," Polly warned him. "If you do, you'll have a jam behind you in a few hours that will lock you in. And you can't get anywhere near the steamboat landing, anyway, except on foot. You'll have to carry your supplies on your backs, no telling how far, when you do find them."

"There's something to think about!" Barnett considered. "Wait here then. Hedges, you come along with me. Frezzell may need help." He started at once toward the town.

"I'll overtake you," Hedges said. "I want to get something out of my wagon."

"How about some of the rest of us going, too?" Lester Lee shouted after Barnett.

"The rest of you stick close around the teams," the wagon master called back. "We don't want to have to hunt for you if we need you sudden. Don't leave here! Don't any of you . . ."

"Look what's coming!" Zenas Rose broke in. "I told you this was no place for women! That's the only wagon yet that's had to give up and head for home! And, of course, it's got a woman in it! Well, that chap's found sense at last."

Mrs. Brush, who had been listening, looked around. "A woman and two children!" she exclaimed. "He's worse off than you are, Colin."

"I guess you and Miss Terry Hut see now what's ahead of you," Rose added. "You join up onto this outfit that's taking the back track, and you'll make a real nice little train."

A wagon drawn by four oxen came up the hill far off the road, which was filled with teams on their way into town. A man walked dejectedly beside the lead pair. A young woman, a boy under ten, and a girl half that age, sat in the driver's seat. The woman's thin, careworn face had a look of contentment.

"Are there many women down there?" Mrs. Brush called, as the wagon was passing.

The man halted his oxen. "I heared say ther's one to ev'ry six, seven men," he answered.

"He ain't goin' back becount o' us!" the woman called from the hooded seat. "Ther's wimminfolks. Wimmin an' young'ns."

"Then, of course, there are trains they can travel with!" cried Colin Brush.

"Some," the man answered. "Whar I counted wrong was comin' on empty, lookin' to load supplies at this place. The way prices is yander, I couldn't buy grub enough to feed the young'ns halfway acrost, leave alone us." He prodded the near ox.

"Wait, Mister!" Polly called. "Will you sell me that stove you have tied on the back?" She hurried after him, Mrs. Brush and Ann following her.

"Come on!" Lester Lee called to Freddie Dascomb. "Let's listen to the dicker." He and some of the other men started after the three women.

"Just a minute, Rose!" Brush said. "I want a word with you. You've gone out of your way several times to say things that my wife could hear, things intended to turn her back from this trip, to frighten her."

"Here's the place for her to turn back, Brush," Rose answered. "There's no argument can convince me . . ."

"I'm not arguing with you," Brush broke in. "I'm telling you. You elect yourself to talk like that again where my wife can hear, or my daughter, and you'll elect yourself to have trouble with me right then."

"This is a fine, big, open country, Mr. Brush," Rose said. "If you're looking for trouble, there's plenty of room here. I'll get the boys to make a ring right here to see you have fair play."

"Some things don't call for just a fist fight," Brush answered. "If you keep on, this will call for more than that. I don't care to find out whether I can beat you with my fists, but I intend to stop you frightening my womenfolks. I mean to stop it!"

Gale Hedges, who was passing, turned back. Three others, who had caught a few words of the argument, stepped up and stood listening.

"I'm with him on that, Zenas," Hedges said. "I've wondered how long it would take for your talk to touch him off."

"The women are coming!" one of the men warned. "Mrs. Brush will hear you."

"She mustn't think you are quarreling!" Hedges spoke very softly. "That would frighten her!"

"I don't give a good . . ."

"All right!" Hedges cried out menacingly, "if you're honing for a fight with me, Rose, I'll give you one!"

"What's this now?" Zenas said in surprise.

"Get your womenfolks away, Brush!" Hedges shouted angrily, and stepping back. "Take off your belt, Rose!" he ordered as he began to unbuckle his own.

Polly and Ann walked up carrying between them a small, lightweight, sheet-iron stove. Eusebia walked behind it, gazing at it with covetous eyes and looking up startled when she heard Hedges again tell Brush to get the women away.

"Oh, please don't fight!" she pleaded. "Come, Colin! Help us carry this stove!"

"If you and Mr. Rose have to fight, Mr. Hedges," Polly said rather lightly, "I hope you'll go away to do it. We want room here to set up my stove near our wagons."

Zenas Rose laughed. "That was a quick one, Gale," he said. "Didn't know you could work so fast."

"Come on, boys," someone urged, and the men moved away.

7

"All right!" Zenas' tone showed that he had calmed down a bit. "You go on after the captain, like Barnett said. Before we fight, what say we get as far away from this place as California?"

"You go down with them, Polly," Mrs. Brush urged, as she picked up the stove. "Maybe you can be a help. While you're gone, I'll bake that big turkey you shot this morning—if only it will go into this little oven. I wonder if it will."

"She wants you to go," Ann whispered, "so she can have this stove of yours all to herself."

"Here, Sebie, I'll carry it for you," Brush offered.

"I'll carry it myself!" the woman answered. "I could hug it! The man who made it is a blacksmith, Colin."

"Don't get into trouble with Rose over anything he may say to me, Mr. Brush." Polly spoke in a low voice. "His talk doesn't worry me."

"Why did you say that?" Brush asked.

"I have good ears, and I was watching, besides," Polly answered. "But Gale Hedges! Whoever would have thought it of him? I'm going to go down to the town with him. But I'll try to get back in time to eat turkey."

VII

LET THE GAL THROUGH

POLLY did not overtake Hedges, nor did she see him on the slope of the hill where hundreds were coming and going, and other hundreds were standing appalled as they stared at the town.

On her way down, she sensed an ominous difference between the men who had just come and the men who had been compelled to remain waiting. Up on the hill, the emigrants who had just arrived gazed spellbound or hurried about asking questions. They wanted to know what the chances were for a quick crossing. Many of them stormed or cursed; but, for the time, they were brothers in misfortune, and all were friendly and willing to impart bits of information.

Down the hill, the girl passed armed and watchful men guarding herds of oxen and droves of mules far from any wagons. The town was a place of noise and confusion, but it was not a place of friendliness, and there seemed to be little talk that was meant for the ears of strangers.

When Polly was deep in the crowd, she heard the mellow whistle of a steamboat, and saw the *La Belle* coming up the river. Ahead of the girl, the narrow lane, usually kept open for travel, filled at once with men hurrying toward the landing. In the midst of the crowd, she saw a tight-lipped, elderly woman sitting alone in a wagon with the name "Happy Days" painted on its cover.

"May I leave my pony here for a while?" Polly asked the woman. She had to repeat the question before the woman turned and looked at her. Then she had to wait for an answer, and all it was, was a nod.

"Tie 'er to a wheel where I can watch 'er," the woman said after Polly had dismounted.

Through streets filled with armed and anxious men, Polly made her way to the boat landing. Everywhere piles of food-stuffs unloaded in haste cluttered the riverside. Polly climbed up on one of these piles. As she stood there, she saw Hedges and Barnett and hailed them.

"There's Brackett!" Hedges cried exultingly, as the steamer drew in.

"Where?"

At the unexpected sound of Captain Frezzell's voice, Polly looked round and saw him. He was trying to make his way through the jam to the wagon master.

"Top deck! Top deck!" she heard Barnett shouting.

"Brooks, too!" Frezzell jerked off his hat and began to wave it. "Jumpin' Jupiter!" he yelled. "That means they've got the freight! They'd never come up together without it!"

The three Rock Island men worked their way through the crowd and stood beside Polly.

"Captain, why can't we get this steamboat, or the one just turning in out yonder, to land our goods on the other side, and our wagons, too?" Barnett asked.

They all looked out to see another steamer coming upstream. Frezzell shook his head. "No steamboat can get anywhere near ·that low bank over there, Joe, for the sand bars," he answered.

"But look what these steamers are doing!" cried the wagon master. "Two of 'em from down river in fifteen minutes, bringing more emigrants and their outfits to be ferried over!"

"Hey, Brackett!" Hedges shouted, "have you got everything?"

"Right with us!" the doctor called back. "But how about getting across? Has the wagon train gone over?"

"Just got here!" Hedges answered.

"Well, that means we've got food to last till fall, and we can camp right here for weeks if we have to," the captain said, "But, tarnation take it, we don't want to have to!"

"Come up here, Frezzell!" Brackett called as the *La Belle* was made fast. "All three of you! We'll do our talking where we can keep an eye on this shipment of ours!"

As soon as the gangplank was lowered, the three went aboard, and no disembarking passengers barred their way.

There were more mules and oxen than there were men on the boat, and the men were unwilling to leave until they could take their possessions with them, but the unloading began promptly.

Polly Kent, still out in the crowd, saw Doctor Brackett lean over the rail, look in her direction, and shout:

"O Bill! Come back here! We've got important things to settle!"

A man who had just come off the *La Belle* waved a hand carelessly, as he stood close beside the girl. He was looking out toward the second steamer, which was turning in with a wood scow lashed alongside. Polly's eyes lighted for a moment when she saw that he was Bill Murillo.

"Later, Doctor!" he answered, "later!" As he turned, he noticed Polly and swept off his hat to her.

His appearance astonished Polly, for he was dressed with the same sporting elegance as when she had seen him in the camp near Rock Island. As then, he was clean shaven and immaculate.

"Well, I hope you didn't think you'd lost me!" he called, as he began to make his way toward her.

"That's so, I haven't seen you, now that I think of it," she answered nonchalantly.

He smiled at that remark. "Didn't the boys tell you, Miss Kent?" he asked. "Then they're no friends of mine. You haven't seen me because I had business down below, and because of a horse I wanted for the trip west—King Cole, that white Arab just coming off the boat."

A white stallion, his fine Mexican saddle and bridle heavily silver mounted, was being led across the gangplank by a Negro.

"What a beautiful animal!" Polly exclaimed.

"Here, Sam, I'll take him," Murillo called. "May King Cole and I walk with you, Miss Kent?"

"Not in this crowd," she answered. "You've no idea how things are here. Five thousand wagons waiting to cross, probably six or seven thousand by now, and only one little ferry."

"Oh! You're in a hurry to be on your way?" He arched his brows at her in feigned surprise. "Then I'll attend to that little matter for you! But first, you'll have to promise to go riding with me. Will you? Promise, and across we go!"

Greatly surprised, she hesitated a moment, then shook her head, "No."

"Won't you ride with me if I get your party and ours across this river tomorrow?"

"All right," she consented, indifferently.

Murillo laughed, then called, "Here, Sam, take care of this horse. Find out where the Rock Island train is, and stay around with it till I come."

"It's yonder, just west of the road at the crest of the hill," Polly told him.

Murillo handed the rein to the Negro, lifted his hat to Polly, and pushed his way through the crowd. Almost under the stern of the *La Belle*, he noticed a boy rowing a small boat about in an eddy. "Hey, Bub!" he called. "Come ashore with that skiff for a minute. I want to talk to you."

"What is it?" the boy asked as he rowed in. "Say, don't get in this boat!"

"I'm already in," was the answer. "Listen! Here's a dollar. Give me a boat ride."

"Gee!" the boy exclaimed. "Lemme have it!" He pocketed the coin and began to ply the oars. "Want me to row you some place?"

"Get out from shore and I'll tell you. That's right, lay to it. Now keep your voice down, Bub . . ."

"Henry," the youngster supplied promptly. "Henry Gill."

"Henry, see that steamboat just coming in with a wood scow lashed alongside? Put me on that scow before the steamer gets to the landing, and there's another dollar for you."

"You'll have to wait till she slows up," the boy answered. "Then we can make it. You steer." He rowed hard for a time. "Steer in more!" he directed breathlessly. "They come up kinda close to shore in this eddy."

"Good work, Henry!" Murillo exclaimed. "I'm going alongside."

"Don't forget that other dollar!" the boy reminded him.

"Here you are!"

"I'll hold 'er while you climb out." The boy drew his oars in and caught hold of the scow.

"Thanks, Henry!"

"Do I row you back?"

"No, I'll stay on the scow. See you again sometime."

Murillo vaulted into the wood boat and landed inside without soiling his clothes or even ruffling them. As he glanced around, he saw an unshaven white man in worn blue overalls and a clean blue shirt standing near by. Several big Negroes were heaving wood into the steamer as fast as they could work.

"You the owner of this scow?" he asked the white man.

"I am that," the white man answered.

"My name's William Murillo."

"Pat Callahan—that's me."

"How much will you charge a day for the use of this boat?"

"Fur what?" Callahan inquired.

"To ferry some wagons across the river. How much if I lease it for three or four days?"

"Can't do that," the owner answered. "I'm contracted fur wood to this line o' steamboats."

"How long can you let me have it?"

"Today—tomorrow—part of next day maybe. But the scow leaks bad—fore an' aft—when she's loaded."

"We'll fix it. I figured that all out coming up the river half an hour ago, Callahan. I watched this scow and figured what we could do. We'll stop the leaks."

"But what about a floor? Ain't none here. Couldn't take no team on 'er, onyway."

"Can't we lay a floor across these stringers?"

"Gorry, I won't stop ye!" Callahan answered. "She'd carry three teams an' a wagon if she had a floor."

"How much?" Bill asked. "How much for the use of the scow till day after tomorrow?"

"She's wurth twenty-foive dollars a day. But after two days I must git 'er home an' load up fur me next boat."

"A hundred dollars for the use of her and for your own services from now till night, and then for two days afterward. How's that?"

"Done!" answered the owner.

"Here's forty dollars on account." Bill handed over some gold pieces.

"That don't take in the black boys," Callahan explained. "They belong to the steamboat."

"Come up to the clerk's office and we'll make out the receipt."

"Don't throw me lines off whin the scow's onloaded!" Callahan shouted. "I'm comin' aboard!"

"All right, Pat!" someone yelled from above.

"Now," Bill said, when they were on the steamer, "is there a boat builder here in St. Joe?"

"Down beyant the ferry," Callahan told him. "Here, Jerry," he said at the door of the clerk's office, "write me a receipt to this man, William Murillo, fur a hundred dollars fur the use o' the scow *and me* till the day after tomorrow night."

"That's easy." The clerk, young, brisk, and obliging, reached for a receipt blank. "One hundred dollars from William Murillo, use of scow and owner's services for two and a half days from noon of this date," he repeated as he wrote. "Now, Pat, sign it."

"I'm trustin' ye to do the writin' safe, Jerry. I nivir put me cross down before without Father O'Fallon runnin' his eye over the paper," said Callahan as he made his mark, "but a hundred cartwheels don't be rollin' downhill into me pocket iv'ry day."

"The scow may be worth it, Mr. Murillo," the clerk said, "but the owner's services will run you a dead loss."

"Some day I'll buy you a drink fur that," Callahan answered, "provided this gentleman don't work the life out o' me."

"Here's the sixty." Murillo handed over the money still due. "Perhaps you'd better sign as a witness."

"Per—haps!" the clerk assented. "There, that's ironclad."

"Thank you!" Murillo said.

"Don't be thankin' 'im!" Callahan interrupted. "He's glad to show off he kin write."

"Come on, I'm in a hurry,"Murillo said, as he moved out to the deck. "We'll float the boat down, as soon as the wood's off."

"Funny river, Mister," Callahan explained. "There's a big eddy that floats you upstream, but you have to be towed down. Three men to a rope ashore'll do that part easy."

Murillo, looking over the crowd at the landing, saw Polly and waved to her. "O Miss Kent!" he shouted.

When she saw him, she held up a hand.

"Come aboard, will you?" he called. "Hurry!"

"I'll hurry as fast as I can!" the girl answered. "There's a pretty big crowd here!"

Callahan leaned over the rail and bellowed. "Let the gal through to the gangplank! Let 'er through there!" He grinned at Murillo. "Keep me usin' only me gintle voice, an maybe I won't be all a dead loss, Mister."

Polly came aboard and hurried toward them.

"Right over here, Miss Kent!" Bill beckoned. "It's out of the crowd here!"

"I'm obliged to you!" she said, smiling at Callahan.

"Oh, could you hear me? I'm surprised at that now!" Callahan took off his hat to her. "Well, I was gittin' paid fur it."

"I've leased a wood scow," Murillo explained.

"That's why I came over here," Polly answered. "I was watching when you got into the rowboat. Captain Frezzell and the others are still on the *La Belle* with Doctor Brackett."

"I expect to be riding with you about tomorrow evening. So, of course, you'll have to come in on this."

"It's good of you!" the girl exclaimed.

"I wish you'd tell Frezzell that I'm taking this new ferry of ours down to the boat builder's. Will you?"

"Yes, but things are pretty desperate here. I think you'd better have me get the others to come," she urged. "Somebody may try to take the scow away from you when everybody sees what it can be used for."

"Good!" Murillo assented. "Tell the captain it will carry a wagon and three yoke of oxen." He handed Polly the receipt.

"I wonder now would they try takin' 'er! It would make a roarin' good fight, that!" Callahan said with relish. "Git your wagons around to the boat yard an' block the place off. Right beyant is a bit of a ravine. Ye kin cut a road down through it to the river easy, if ye have plinty o' men."

"We've plenty of men," Murillo assured him. "We'll have to make a good many repairs to the scow before we can use it, Miss Kent. It leaks, and we will have to have a floor put in."

"Don't you know that Colin Brush is a boat builder?" the girl exclaimed. "That was his trade in Detroit."

"Get him down there then, will you? I'll stay with the scow. Tell the captain to hurry over here before she's unloaded."

"I'll tell him," Polly said.

"Good-by, Miss!" Callahan called after her.

"Good-by!" she answered, as she was hastening away.

She lost no time getting off the steamer, but she found the river bank crowded with men. "Let me pass, please!" she kept repeating as she forced her way among them. "Let me pass! I want to get through to the *La Belle!* O Captain Frezzell! Pshaw! He doesn't hear me!"

"Captain Frezzell!" shouted a man at her side. "Lady here wants you! Was that the name, Miss? Frezzell?"

"Yes! Now he sees me!"

Frezzell came to the rail of the upper deck, and Polly climbed on a pile of unloaded freight where she would be near him and where few others could hear the conversation.

"Captain," she said, "Mr. Murillo has leased a wood scow for the rest of today, tomorrow, and the day after."

"What's that?" cried the captain. "A wood scow, you say?"

"Not so loud, Captain!" she warned. "He wants all of you over there right away—beside that other steamer."

"A scow we can use as a ferry?" the captain whispered.

"Yes, and he wants you there so no one can steal it from him! He wants the whole train down at the boat builder's!"

"Hallelujah!" the captain exclaimed. "Boys . . ."

"Oh, don't try to tell them in front of all this crowd!" the girl cried.

"Come on, boys! Don't ask questions!"

"Don't you want all the men and the wagons to go down there?" Polly asked the captain as he was leaving the rail.

"Can you fetch 'em? You got your pony?"

"Yes, Captain."

"Tell Zenas Rose it's my orders! And hurry! Make time! This may be our salvation, if we can put it through!"

It took Polly ten minutes to reach her pony, and a much longer time to get through the rest of the crowd.

Out where the incoming trains were halting, she saw several of the South Bend men, with Butler among them. He lifted his hat to her, and she returned his greeting. Just as she was guiding her pony through an opening toward the road, she heard a name and a voice that startled her.

"What you want, Tasker?" someone shouted.

"Plenty!"

The answering voice was that of Webb Tasker, who had caused the trouble at Sintan's ferry. Polly turned and saw him. As a dozen or more hard-faced fellows gathered about him, she heard him say excitedly: "There's a party got hold of a scow, an' we can grab 'er! They're floatin' 'er down to the boat yard! Look whur she's jest swung out from the steamboat! Git your wagons together! We'll run 'em down to whur the scow's to land, rush 'er, an' take 'er! They're a slick bunch that's tryin' to beat everybody to the ferries by dirty tricks! But their train ain't in yet!"

Polly could not hear what the others answered, but she could see their faces as they stood huddled around Tasker, talking now in low voices. In a moment, however, she saw them scatter.

VIII

THE MISSOURI TO CROSS

POLLY sat watching Tasker until he was lost in the crowd. She knew she had little chance to get word to the men on the wood scow while they were out in the stream. She also knew that a warning received by them after they had landed might be too late. So she swung about and rode back toward the South Bend wagons. Now and then one of the few women she saw turned to stare, but the men seldom gave her a second glance. Here at the frontier, in this throng of dismayed gold seekers drawn from every class and occupation, even a pretty girl in a suit of deerskins, and riding astride, attracted no great attention.

"Mr. Butler!" she called, as she drew near him. "O Mr. Butler! stop your train, please, and hold it till I tell you something."

"Sorry!" he answered. "Can't stop now! We'll have to get ourselves out of this jam before we're blocked in. We made a mistake in coming down here. I hope your people were wiser."

"Is that man Tasker a member of your train again?" she asked.

"No, and he never will be!"

"Then don't let your wagons turn back!" she urged. "Stop them!"

Butler stood looking at her with narrowed eyes before he came to a decision, but he made up his mind quickly. "Wait, men!" he shouted. "Just for a minute, till I hear what's on this young lady's mind." He stepped forward briskly. "Miss Kent, what is it?"

"We've a boat! A boat!" Polly whispered. "And Tasker is rounding up a pack of desperate men to steal it from us before the slow oxen can get down from the hill. I just heard him making his plans. And the Rock Island men don't know it, not even the ones on the scow."

"Where do we come in?" Butler asked. "You want us to help the Rock Island outfit?"

"Are you friends with them, after what happened two or three weeks ago?" the girl asked.

"Friends? Why not?" Butler answered. "None of our crowd blames your people. And if it comes to a fight with Tasker, we'll all be for it. Provided, of course," he added quickly, "that it also means a chance for our train to cross the river at once, instead of waiting heaven knows how long!"

Polly leaned over to whisper to Butler.

"I don't know whether it means that or not," the girl told him frankly. "It may mean a chance to cross, and it may not, Mr. Butler. They're to have the scow till day after tomorrow night. It will carry a wagon and three teams at a time, mules or oxen, but it will have to be mended first. It leaks and it has no floor yet."

"Two days!" Butler still spoke softly, but Polly saw that he was excited. "Both trains ought to cross in two days! On a chance of it, we'll deal with you, Miss Kent. I'm acting captain of this train—have been for the last ten minutes—and I speak for the train."

"I've no authority to bargain," Polly explained. "I'm not even a member of the Rock Island party. You'll have to bargain with the men, but they've promised to take me over with them—Mr. Brush and me."

"Where are they?"

"I can tell you where they'll be," she answered. "But you'll have to give me your word to do just what I tell you and to move quickly."

"If it's something we *can* do, and is halfway reasonable, you have the promise," Butler said.

"There's a boat builder's place below the ferry, on beyond the center of the town and the edge of the jam. I saw it this morning. It stands alone, and I know you can't miss it. Get your train down there just as soon as you possibly can, and spread it out so you'll block off the whole space. Keep everyone except us from getting in. The man that owns the boat said that a road can easily be made there."

"Wait, men!" Butler cried. "Swing out of this crowd, but skirt on past it! We're not going back to the hill!"

"But their train . . . you'll have to let their wagons through —and Mr. Brush's and mine—so we can be the first to cross," the girl said.

"We'll do that!" Butler assured her. "But where can I find your men right now? We can't let someone else make a bargain with them before we have a chance to."

"They're on the scow, there beyond the steamboats."

"The one pulling into the stream?"

"Yes, and the only one anywhere, I reckon, Mr. Butler."

"Where are they going?"

"Down to the boat builder's."

"You heard that, Honus!" Butler spoke to a man who had been listening, the man in an army hat with a hole through the crown which a bullet had made. "Get word to all our drivers. And keep them moving. You lead the way—and find the boat builder's. Spread the wagons around well back from the river, just as Miss Kent said, and keep everybody out till the Rock Island train comes down."

"I'll handle it, Lieutenant," Honus answered and turned away. But Butler held him by the arm an instant.

"I'm going to follow that scow, and see that no one gets a bid in for it ahead of us," he explained.

"I'm obliged to you!" Polly was breathless.

"I hope we're going to be the grateful ones, grateful to you," Butler answered. "Don't you think you'd better go hurry your own party to the boat builder's? We may have a hot war on our hands all of a sudden. But we're seventy-four men, all armed with rifles, and we'll hold things tight till your people come."

"I'll fetch them," Polly promised.

Keiēta, the deep-chested, smoke-colored Indian pony, had heavy, strong legs, but very trim hoofs and pasterns and surprising speed for her size. Toughened by weeks of hard travel, she made the hill easily at a fast run, slid to a stop beside Polly's wagon, drew one deep breath after the bridle rein had been tossed over her head, and stood quietly when the girl left her.

"Captain's orders!" Polly cried. "He wants the whole train down there! Just beyond the town! I'll show you where! We've a boat! And we're going across!"

The men, who had been silently listening, began to exclaim. "To cross? Today you mean?" several asked excitedly.

"Don't know when," Polly answered, going to her team, which had been unhitched but not unharnessed. "Tomorrow, more likely. But no time for explanations now. We have to get down there. Tasker is rounding up men to take the boat, to steal it from us!"

"Tasker!"

She heard the name repeated many times in quick, angry sentences. At once there was a great deal of shouting and commotion.

"Did you grab that boat for us, too, Miss Kent?" one of the men called to her.

"No, it was Mr. Murillo, the minute he got off the boat which came up from St. Louis," the girl answered. "And

Doctor Brackett and Mr. Brooks came, too, with all the supplies."

"The way you came tearing along," Brush said, "I thought something had happened! How did you get us in on that new ferry this time? Or are we in?"

"Yes, we're to cross," was all Polly said.

"Get to your wagons!" Zenas Rose ordered, though the train was already moving.

"It's all right, though," Polly cried. "The South Bend men have joined up with us to hold Tasker and his crowd off! They're already down there."

"Bully for South Bend!" someone shouted.

Polly heard Rose growl, "All I don't like is Frezzell sending us orders by a squaw! Couldn't he 'ave sent somebody else?" Then she heard one of the men snap back, "You better talk soft about that girl around here just now, Zenas! She knows a heap more about the road ahead of us than we do!"

"Polly," Brush asked in a low voice, "are you sure we're joined in on this? There can't be any mistake about that, can there?"

"No mistake. We're to cross with them," she told him. "And they need you right off to help repair the boat. It leaks, and there's no floor in it yet."

"Sebie," Brush called to his wife, busy with his oxen, "get set quick to move along!"

"But what am I to do with this turkey?" Mrs. Brush cried in dismay. "It's in the oven! And this stove's piping hot!"

"Leave it! Leave everything! We can't stop for things like that!" her husband shouted impatiently. "Get into the wagon! You and Ann!"

"Leave my stove?" Polly was indignant. "Indeed not! There'll be nothing more important than well-cooked food on this trip, Mr. Brush!"

"Thunder and lightning!" he exclaimed. "I thought *you* were sensible! Are we going to California? Or are we staying here to cook turkey?"

"Don't you leave it!" Eusebia pleaded. "It's as good a stove as ever I used! And it takes so little firewood! It's a mighty sight better than cooking over a campfire!"

"Mother, you go along with him," Ann urged. "He never says 'thunder and lightning' unless he's plum provoked. I'll stay and help Polly."

Mrs. Brush climbed to the wagon seat, but reached over it, then got down at once, and went back toward the stove, unfolding two big towels as she walked. She opened the oven door, pulled the pan out onto the ground, lifted the turkey by the legs with one towel and wrapped the other around it.

"There," she said. "I've got the turkey. That leaves you only the stove and the pan to bring. Just empty the grease out. Don't you leave that stove, girls! We'll never get another like it!"

The men swung their wagons back into the road. Polly lifted off the lids of the stove, and with her foot overturned it to dump out the fire. "Whew!" She whistled. "That's hot!"

"Do you think it will take very long to cool?" Ann asked anxiously.

"Let me do this!" Suddenly, one of the Rock Island party, a young man whose name the girls had never heard, edged in and quickly took the legs off the stove.

"The legs go into the firepot, and the lids, the pan, and the three short lengths of pipe go in the oven when the stove is ready to be hung on the wagon," Polly explained.

"You go steer the train down! They want you! I'll fetch your stove along," the young man said. "Easy to run a few turns of this stout wire around it even if it is hot. And I've a place to hang it behind my wagon where it can't bang against things."

"Well," Polly answered, "for all your kindness, you've a piece of that turkey coming. You're going to have a piece, Mr. . . ."

"Just holler *Jacquin*, Pierre Jacquin, when the turkey's being passed around. And either black meat or white meat, or even a little of both will do fine." He and the girls laughed.

"Will you drive my ponies again, Ann?" Polly asked.

"You know I'd love to!" was the eager answer.

"In the saddle it will be easier for me to warn the train away from badly crowded places."

In a few moments they were all lined up in the road on their way down the hill. The oxen were prodded hard, and there was much impatient shouting to speed them, but even at their liveliest, they traveled slowly.

Several members of the party, carrying rifles, walked well in advance of the train. To them Polly occasionally returned to report on conditions ahead. When they had passed around the more congested part of the town and were approaching the boat yard, they could see signs of trouble. There the South Bend wagons were drawn up in an incomplete half circle. On the side toward the town the line ended more than a hundred feet from the edge of the river bank. In the space where there were no wagons, men with rifles stood facing what looked like a dozen mule-drawn prairie schooners which had come to a standstill on a very rough piece of ground. From many directions people were flocking toward them.

"They're holding off Tasker's friends!" Polly reported. "And we're not to go in where the fight is threatening, but clear around on the other side. There a wagon will swing out of the circle to let us in."

"Good headwork for someone!" Rose exclaimed.

"Lieutenant Butler!" Polly answered.

"Lieutenant?" Rose repeated.

"He served in the Mexican War, so the man he had waiting outside with a message told me. He left the gap in the circle on purpose, to lure Tasker there out of the way, and where they can be held off easiest."

"Let's go over and surround that band!" Rose urged. "Come on, boys!"

"Lieutenant Butler wants us to get our wagons inside his ring and to tend to our own job!" Polly interrupted.

"He send that word?"

"That," Polly answered, "and also for us to keep in close formation, so that no one can wedge across our course and cut off part of our train."

"Go tell everybody to prod up and keep close together," Rose ordered one of the men.

"May have gosh awful good practice here, Zenas, for when the Indians pester us," someone suggested.

Zenas laughed. "Drop back then," he said. "Practice guarding your own outfit, each one of you, till you get inside."

Some of the men waited for their cattle to come up to them; others hastened to take their assigned places.

As they swung around the half circle, all of them could hear Tasker's voice. The drivers could see him, and they could see Butler, too, whom he seemed to be threatening. But when Butler spoke, they could not hear what he said.

The wood scow lay at the water's edge, a half-dozen men aboard her working, and paying no attention to the disturbance. Captain Frezzell, on seeing the Rock Island train, did straighten up and wave his hat, but a moment later he was helping to lift a heavy floor plank aboard. Others were shoveling bark out of the scow.

"Drive in right here!" a South Bend man shouted.

The mule train was drawn up, the wagons all headed toward the river, and there was not room enough to pass between them. But the one to which the mules were still hitched moved out of the line and opened a way through.

"Unyoke and tie up your oxen!" the South Bend man said as the train was turning in. "We're going to hold this place. And your captain wants eight yoke of oxen down at the river in a hurry to drag that scow that's ready for calking up the bank."

"How about us helping you beat off that Tasker outfit?" Rose called.

"You men get the ferry ready! That's your job! We'll take care of Tasker! We've got the promise of that boat as soon as you're all over on the other side. And unless we have it two hours before dark tomorrow, there won't be time to get our whole train across. Overton's my name."

"Mine's Zenas Rose. Lester, you and Freddie swing off your wagons and unhitch. Get eight yoke down and yank that scow out of the water in a rush. That's work for you for not driving back at the end of the line where you belong!"

"Keep clear of the stretch that's being staked off there!" Overton shouted. "We're going to cut a road down right there!"

Polly had dismounted, and both she and Ann were busy with the ponies. She could see the boat and the men at work on it, and she could also see other men crowding about it pleading with Captain Frezzell to ferry them and their wagons across the river. A dozen South Bend men with rifles barring Tasker's way into the enclosure were also discernible, but Polly could not see anything beyond them except some mule teams and the tops of several wagon covers. She saw the men guarding the gap suddenly swing up their rifles. There was an instant of quiet, then threatening talk again outside.

"Is it that man Tasker who's talking?" Ann asked.

"Yes!" Polly answered. "Listen!"

"I wish you boys would bring back that stove," Mrs. Brush called.

"In just a minute," Jacquin shouted.

"And that's final!" Tasker bellowed. "Out of our way, or we come throwin' lead!"

For the first time, Butler spoke so that Polly and the others could hear what he said. Unhurriedly, and in a voice without vibrance, he asked, "Honus, are you all set?"

"Yes, Lieutenant!" The speaker's tones were muffled. "We've got 'em singled out and covered from inside our wagons!"

"If any man makes a move to use a gun, we've got to shoot! Any man except Tasker," Butler added. "Tasker's talk puts him where he's going to draw on me. He's to have a fair chance, Honus, before and after. Understand that?"

"Yes, Lieutenant!"

"Tasker, nobody's covering you," Butler said. "It's all between you and me. I'll wait till you reach for your gun."

There was a moment of silence, then a single pistol shot rang out.

Three men were driving stakes to mark the place for the roadway where a small ravine ran down to the water.

"Come on!" cried one of them. "Let's see what's happened!"

They dropped the stakes and started to run toward the place near the river bank where there were no wagons.

"Jump back on your own job!" Overton called to them. "Your job's to get that road ready!"

Brush had tied his cattle without waiting to take off the yokes, and was on his way to the river when he heard the shot.

"You women get into our wagon and stay there!" he shouted. "That sounds like trouble starting!"

"Come on, Ann!" Eusebia called. "Get in, you and Polly!"
In a lower tone, she added, "He'll worry if you don't, Honey."
Then louder, "All right, Colin!"

Brush went on, but kept looking back until Ann had climbed
in.

"Mind if I set it down right here?" Pierre Jacquin asked as
he came in great haste, bringing the stove. "I want to get out
there and see what's happening before everything's over."
Then dropping the stove, he hurried across to the ring of men
who had the rifles.

Polly, who had been wanting to see, hurried after him. But
Eusebia listened, gazed for a moment toward the scene of the
disturbance, and then looked at the stove.

"I guess there's no trouble after all, Ann," she decided, and
began to climb down from the seat. "I want to set that stove
up. I've got the knack of it, and I'd love to do it."

Butler was still outside the wagon-ringed corral. Beyond
him but facing him, Polly saw a number of men who were
carrying rifles but making no move to use them. A dozen
others of the Tasker party, drivers up behind their mules,
were watching, with only the reins in their hands. Tasker lay
stretched on the ground, a man stooping over him.

"When the doctor is through," Butler said in a very loud
tone, "we'll take the names of all you men as witnesses. You'll
be held up here a few weeks, anyway, by the lack of ferry service, so the delay of a trial won't make any difference to you."

"Who said so!" cried a bearded old fellow in the crowd which
had gathered on the rise of ground behind Tasker's party.

"Besides, I didn't see nuthin'." He turned and started off, elbowing everybody out of the way.

"Me either!" a ringing voice piped up. "Saw nothing . . . and heard nothing!" With that the speaker followed after the first man. And at once many others turned, then hurried off.

"How is he, Doctor?" Butler asked.

"A hole in his right shoulder," the man beside Tasker answered, "where the bullet went clean through. But I'm not equipped to attend him; I'm driving a mule team now."

"Put 'im in my wagon," a friend of Tasker's suggested eagerly. "I'll take 'im somewhars."

"I want the names of all these witnesses!" Butler demanded again in a loud voice.

"He's saying that to scatter the crowd," Jacquin whispered to Polly.

"How will that scatter them?" she asked.

"Calling for witnesses? Pretty near telling 'em they'll never get to California if they admit they saw the shooting," Jacquin chuckled. "That fellow Butler learned something about being held up as a witness, Miss Kent, back there at Sintan's ferry. He don't want to be delayed for any trial his own self."

"Why, they're all leaving," Polly exclaimed.

"Leaving!" Jacquin repeated. "Look at 'em go! Kiting out like Tasker's friends. They don't want any of that witness business either."

Several of the men who had come with Tasker were swinging their teams and making for the rear. Now there was no one in the space where the crowd had been.

"Say, that Butler's a smart fellow!" Jacquin whispered. "But then he's a lawyer, and I suppose a good lawyer just wouldn't miss that trick, would he? I'll bet there's fifty men of his own party that he could get for witnesses, and he knows it."

"It *is* funny, the way everybody hurried away," Polly answered.

"Here, take ahold with me an' hist 'im in!" someone called. "Git 'im to a doctor, or we'll never git out o' here!"

Tasker was placed in the wagon and was driven rapidly away. The other wagons belonging to his friends, as well as the friends themselves, were already vanishing.

Accompanied by the doctor, Butler turned and entered the enclosure.

"Lieutenant, I suppose I should have got my kit and worked over him," the doctor said, "but I didn't want to keep that crowd hanging around here."

"That, of course, was the most important thing," Butler answered. "I had to shoot in self-defense, but I aimed at the shoulder. Will he pull through?"

"Oh, land, yes! With any kind of care."

"We didn't see anything, Lieutenant," Jacquin asserted.

"It seems there weren't any witnesses." Butler smiled.

Polly saw that his clean-shaven face was ashen, that his nostrils spread widely each time he breathed, but that he stood quietly and spoke quietly.

"I'm sorry!" she said to him.

"Sorry?" He looked at her inquiringly.

"I got you into it."

"You got us all into a very good bargain," Butler answered. "Thank you, Miss Kent! We're to have the boat tomorrow for the hundred dollars they've already paid, and half the cost of the repairs. They are fair-minded, as you said."

Polly had classified Butler as a short, rather slender man. As they talked, she was surprised to find herself looking up to him. Previously when they had conversed, she had not noticed how lean and strong and alertly poised he was, but she noticed now. She liked his eyes—gray they were—and a girl could meet their direct gaze without embarrassment. They gave fire to a face that could have appeared cold and too controlled. Butler had not followed the forty-niners' fashion for red shirts, but wore one of dark blue. Though there was nothing in his attire especially to attract attention, Polly felt that he was a man one would not forget.

"Miss Kent, Doctor Vanander," Butler broke the silence.

The girl in turn introduced Jacquin, and the two men shook hands.

"Careful!" Butler cautioned softly. "Doctor, tell the boys in the wagons not to show their rifles. There comes a man with a badge. From his looks, he's not as open-minded as our friend Sheriff Cole was back in Iowa."

Doctor Vanander moved away without haste. Polly saw him stop beside the nearest wagon, stand there a moment, and then go on to the next one. She knew that he was passing the word along. In a moment, Butler turned as if to follow him.

"Wait there!" the man with the badge shouted. "Who did that shooting? What happened?"

"It was not in our corral," Butler answered. "We were just talking about it."

"Then you're the first that has!" The officer eyed the three suspiciously. "Did you see it?"

"It was outside our enclosure, officer," Butler said.

"I know the crowd was, but how about the shot?"

"Outside," Butler answered again.

"How about them men with rifles? Your men?"

"Our corral guards." Butler called to the men, some of whom were only a few steps away, "Did you see what happened, any of you, outside there?"

"Saw nothing—heard nothing," one of them answered with a very grave expression.

"See?" the officer exclaimed in disgust. "There you are! More o' the dumb an' the blind! An' I suppose *you* didn't see nothin', either!"

"Yes, I did," Butler returned quickly. "I saw several prairie schooners out there. Near one of them a man was lying on the ground. Someone lifted him into one of the wagons. I heard someone say he'd been shot in the shoulder, but that it didn't look serious. I knew he wasn't one of our men, though."

"How'd you know he wasn't one o' your men?"

"They all had tasks assigned them and they were busy inside here. At present we're under a kind of military discipline."

"How did it come you went outside then?"

"I'm acting captain of the train. I heard a lot of noise and went out to see."

"Another party try to break in on you?" the officer asked.

"Another party came in," Butler told him. "A train from Rock Island, Illinois. Those oxen are theirs. We're driving mules. But the other train didn't break in, Sheriff. We're in a way joined up with them for a few days, with the people from Rock Island."

"I'll talk to 'em then."

"The captain and most of his men are at the scow," Butler replied. "I'll go down with you. I believe you're going down, too, Miss Kent."

"Yes," Polly answered.

"What did *you* see?" the officer asked her, as they started toward the river.

"I got there in time to see a man lifted into the back of a wagon," she told him, "and to see the people all go away."

"How did it come you went out there? Wasn't you set to any work? Or don't the women figure in on this military discipline business?"

"I'd just driven in with the Rock Island train."

"Oh," the officer exclaimed. "Well, that seems to check. I seen that train go in. An' the shootin' must o' been down outside in the swale, like you said. If it was up here on the level, I'd o' seen it, fer I was lookin'."

He, Butler, and the girl were approaching the river bank, and could see and hear the men at work on the scow.

"You don't need to come any farther with us unless you wish to," Butler whispered to Polly. "I wanted to let him get through asking you questions, so he'd not remember you afterward and go hunting about your train."

"What they yokin' oxen to the flatboat for?" the officer, who was a few steps ahead, asked.

"To pull it out on the bank so they can calk its leaks," Butler told him. "We'd better stop here a minute or we'll be in their way."

The two ox drivers began to shout at their teams; men hurried up, each carrying a small log which he placed as a roller under the front of the slowly ascending scow. The cattle, straining and floundering, dragged the boat up the bank until its blunt ends were out of the water.

Davis Dean, a steamboat calker from the Bailey and Boyle shipyard in Rock Island, got under one end of the scow with material and tools for calking. A dozen or more men who had been carrying heavy floor planks to the edge of the water changed their course so they could shove the planks aboard the scow in its new position. The moment the oxen stopped pulling, three Rock Island men, whose work of laying the new deck had been interrupted, again began to drive in spikes with their heavy, long-handled hammers.

On each side of the craft two men were rigging extra oarlocks; and close beside Butler, two others had begun to make a pair of long oars.

The officer stepped up to Gale Hedges, who was standing on the bank gazing toward the steamer landing, "Well," he began, "did you happen to see that shooting?"

"Don't bother me!" Hedges answered angrily. "I'm watching for a signal." Then turning to Polly, "If you see Doctor Brackett lift his hat over there on the *La Belle*, Miss Kent, tell me."

"Mighty busy outfit here all of a sudden!" the officer remarked.

"What part of the boat?" Polly asked.

"There it is!" Hedges shouted. "Hey, Frezzell! We're to load our supplies on the scow right from the deck of the steamer! I got the signal!"

"You've only an hour to calk those leaks!" Frezzell called. "We'll ease the boat back then and row her up to the *La Belle*. Put all the planks aboard, boys. We'll keep right on laying deck while we're taking on freight."

"That's a timesaver!" Hedges said joyously, "not having to tote the freight from the steamboat to the wagons and then haul it all the way around here through that crowd."

"I'm talkin' to you!" the officer called after him angrily, as he started away.

"Mr. Hedges, a deputy sheriff is speaking to you," Butler interrupted.

"I want to know if you seen that shootin'."

"What shooting?" Hedges inquired in unfeigned surprise.

The officer stared at him a moment, then at Butler. "You're so daft to git to California, you gold-diggers, they kin shoot a man down right next you without you battin' an eye!" he said. "An' what good'll it do you? What'll gainin' a day or a week at this crossin' count you? You'll have to lay up two, three weeks on yon side o' the river waitin' fer the Lord to grow grass fer your stock to feed on anyhow! What's the all-fired hurry?"

IX

DEVIL TAKE THE HINDMOST

AT ONE in the afternoon, the scow was taking supplies off the steamboat; at two, it was back at the boat builder's. By midnight the road had been finished: the scow, with deck laid and two new oars and oarlocks, was ready for use as a ferry, and there was an apron over which the wagons could be hauled aboard. About half the men of both companies remained on guard the rest of the night. Next morning, the first trip was begun at the graying of dawn with two yoke of oxen, Polly's three ponies, and her light spring wagon as the first load.

The river, which was about a third of a mile wide, had a high bank on the eastern side and a wide sandbar on the west. Nearly a fourth of a mile above the steamboat landing an eddy ran upstream and then struck the main current, which there tended rather to the western side.

A shout went up from the thousands already out on the bank watching, as the scow passed the landing with all four oars going. Polly stepped off onto the sandbar on the other side of the river eight minutes after leaving the boat builder's.

There had not been time to get an apron ready for the bow, but after the horses and the oxen had been taken off, two heavy oak planks, fifteen inches wide and two feet long, were laid from the deck to the land the same distance apart as the wheels, and down these the crew rolled the wagons.

Six horsemen and thirty other men were waiting to cross to St. Joseph, and the Rock Islanders took them aboard, charging fifty cents for the horses and ten cents each for the men.

By three in the afternoon, when the South Bend company took possession of the scow after paying Captain Frezzell a hundred dollars, and half the sixty dollars spent for repairs, the last wagon of the train, as well as two tons of hay and thirty bushels of barley, was on the western side of the river.

As the Rock Island men had collected forty dollars in ferry charges, their crossing of the Missouri not only cost them nothing, but also gave them a profit of ten dollars. Most of them had worked two days and a night without sleep and they were worn out. They made no attempt to move their wagons and oxen off the bar, but rolled up in their blankets there, too weary even to think of posting guards.

At a little after five next morning, Brush came to the place where Polly's ponies were standing hitched, and led them up behind his schooner. "The road ahead meanders five miles through timbered bottom land just to get up on the bench

where the prairie begins," he said. "Did you hear the talk of
the men going back to town? It's five miles of mud, most of
it belly-deep; and you can't travel as fast as the oxen. They're
made for heavy hauling."

Rigging a chain to his rear axle, he fastened it to the tongue
and then to the front axle of her wagon. "We'll help you
wallow through," he said, as he caught up his goad.

Polly looked at his load, fearing that it alone was heavy
enough to bog his cattle down. She knew that his wagon was
full, for at the boat builder's he had stored in it six hundred
pounds of flour in bags, five hundred pounds of clear side-
bacon, a hundred pounds of hard bread or crackers, a hundred
pounds of dried tongues, a hundred pounds of dried venison
hams bought in St. Louis at three cents a pound, eighty pounds
of sugar, a bag of green coffee, and a big sack of salt.

The women stayed in the wagons, and Brush floundered
beside his steers to guide and prod them. The road was the
worst Polly had ever seen, and Brush and the teams were
exhausted when, soon after two in the afternoon, they arrived
at the bluff.

Half an hour later the first wagon of the ox train passed
where they were resting. The Rock Island men had met thirty
mounted Indians in the bottom land; and on the high ground,
Captain Frezzell, for the first time, ordered the train drawn up
in a circle. He warned that in going into camp hereafter, the
men must always form an enclosure in which the cattle
might be held safe and the men give battle if they were attacked
at night by Indians.

Polly heard the order given to leave no gaps anywhere in the enclosure, except a narrow opening through which the men and oxen could go and come between the first wagon to stop and the last to take position. She saw Brush, who was watching this maneuver, turn away disappointed. She knew he had been hoping that he and she would be asked to join the train now that the men were friendly and could count on them not only to keep the pace but to be helpful.

His disappointment surprised her. The possibility of their being invited to join had not occurred to her, for the vote back beyond the Mississippi had been so decisively *no women* that she had accepted it as final. But when she saw the corral formed, with its narrow passageway between wagon number one and wagon number seventeen, she was sorry for Colin.

Brush prodded his oxen and drove on. It was not until he was far beyond the Rock Island train that he halted to unhitch.

On the table-land west of St. Joseph, at the edge of the Great Plains, more than four hundred wagons, the animals held close about them, were waiting for the new grass to spring up. The mules and oxen all looked as if they were much in need of rest. Some of them had been cleaned after their hard hauling in the river bottom, and were well cared for, but most of the men were still in their muddy clothes.

A small train, which had used the old ferry, soon passed the site which Brush had chosen, and stopped not far away. About a dozen of the South Bend wagons came through from the river an hour or two before dark. On beyond the last train, they swung into a half circle, which would be completed when the others of the party reached the bluff next day.

Lieutenant Butler rode over to Polly's wagon on a deep-chested young bay gelding, both he and his horse splattered and plastered with mud. Polly and Ann had washed, given their clothes a thorough cleaning, and had finished their chores for the day. Butler smiled at their neat appearance.

"In the fuss and hurry of holding the boat and getting it ready," he said after he had dismounted, "I hadn't time to tell you how grateful we all are in our camp, Miss Kent, for the unexpected chance you gave us to cross the river."

"It was just as lucky for us!" Polly exclaimed. "Your being where I could reach you was a godsend!" She introduced him to Mrs. Brush and Ann. Colin and he were already acquainted.

"Don't you want to wash too?" Sebie asked. "We've lots of hot water. We've had supper and done the dishes, so we won't need much water."

Butler looked at the steaming kettle. "It wouldn't do any good," he said regretfully. "I have to go back tonight to see about getting the other wagons up here tomorrow. Thank you—but I may as well stick to the mud and not bother you."

While they were talking, men were coming and going on all sides. One rode up on a white stallion, dismounted a few steps away, and approached Polly, hat in hand. Both horse and man were so spick and span—so carefully groomed—that Butler observed them intently.

"Good evening, Mr. Murillo!" the girl said, as the new arrival bowed to her.

"Are you ready?" Murillo asked in a low tone.

For a moment she stood silent, looking at him.

"Lieutenant Butler," she said, "are you and Mr. Murillo acquainted?"

The men smiled as they shook hands.

"It was Mr. Murillo who thought of getting the wood scow for us all," Polly said.

"It was Mr. Murillo that I closed the deal with for that scow," Butler told her. "As soon as he learned that Miss Kent approved it, the matter was settled."

For a moment Polly did not look at either man, but turned to Mrs. Brush and Ann, who had withdrawn a little and introduced Murillo to them.

"I see your pony is saddled and ready," he said, smiling at Polly after he had spoken to Ann and her mother.

'Yes," she answered, without telling the promise she had made to this man. With Lieutenant Butler standing there she suddenly felt not at all inclined to discuss it.

But Lieutenant Butler said at once, "If you've an engagement to go for a ride, Miss Kent . . ."

And smilingly lifting his hat, he bowed a little formally, mounted, and rode away in the direction of the river.

Polly started for her pony, but Murillo was there ahead of her and would have given her a hand in mounting, but she declined his help.

"It's different, thank you," she smiled, "this riding astride. I'd like to go through the camp if you're willing. I haven't seen it yet."

She went easily into the saddle and, with the Brushes gazing after her in silent wonderment, headed her pony into the north, the stallion keeping pace at her side.

"This is the road we'll have to travel as soon as the grass is high enough," she began conversation. "We may as well see what the country ahead is like."

There were no settlements this side of the Missouri River, but the two passed a few wagons and farther on a small train which had ventured out from the encampment. After that the open prairie with not a living thing in sight stretched ahead.

The girl rode fast, purposely making conversation difficult. Suddenly Murillo caught her bridle rein and drew both horses to a stop.

"Polly," he said, "you've paid your debt. But can't we go a bit more slowly and get acquainted?"

Polly, pleased by his thoughtfulness, smiled for the first time. "All right," she agreed, and they returned at an easy pace. She found Murillo full of pleasantries and entertaining talk. Presently she realized that she was enjoying herself and getting on with him very well indeed.

He kept looking at her as if he thought her amusing.

"Miss Polly," Murillo said at length, in a tone of severity, "did you tell the good folks you are traveling with why I was able to dash up and sweep you off with me?"

"No," she answered shortly, then in a moment continued, "I think they were very much surprised, Mr. Murillo."

"You should have told them!" he scolded. "Or I should. Why didn't you?"

"Do you want your friends to know that you'd have let them stay in St. Joe—stay fuming and fussing there all summer, perhaps—if you hadn't tried to show a girl from down the Wabash how smart you are?"

"Now, that would have been too bad, wouldn't it?" he laughed.

And Polly, in sudden realization that his bargain with her had been merely an afterthought, that he would have carried out the plan even though she had refused the ride, blushed deeply.

The daylight was still lingering as they turned off the road at the moment toward the two closely parked wagons, Polly's and the Brushes'.

"O Mrs. Brush!" Murillo called. "To keep a promise, Miss Polly has just taken a ride with me. And I'll bet she hasn't told you, has she? I wheedled a promise from her to go for this ride if I got you people all across, and when she promised, I went right after the wood scow I'd been planning for hours to hire!"

Polly saw that his eyes were lighted with mischief. The joke was on her: she had not been the inspiration for his cleverness as she had thought! He had learned down the river of the crowds wherever there were ferries, and had made the entire plan to get the scow before he met her. For an instant she was furious at herself; then she burst into laughter.

Murillo lingered a moment, then rode away.

The next morning, Polly saddled her pony as soon as she thought the women in the camp were likely to be alone at their wagons.

"Is Mr. Murillo coming?" Ann asked shyly.

The question embarrassed the older girl. "No," she answered, "I believe not."

As Polly rode away, she avoided the trains in which there happened to be any men who knew her. Some distance from them, she saw a woman working over a campfire in a well-kept enclosure. This woman seemed very neat in appearance. The pots and pans she was using were clean and carefully placed for her convenience, and the wagon beside her was new. The oxen staked near by seemed to be in good condition, and were feeding contentedly. Polly rode up, dismounted, and asked, "Do you think your train would take any more women?"

"No," the woman answered in alarm and with a quick glance about her.

"Would you and your husband care to join up with our two wagons?" Polly inquired. "There are four of us, a man and his wife, their daughter, and me."

"Don't talk where them men can hear!" the woman whispered. "We don't go in for swappin' round. He's turrible set on stickin' to this train. An' he's wishin' he hadn't brung me." Picking up a kettle, she disappeared around her wagon, thus ending the conversation.

That day Polly talked to nineteen women scattered among eleven different trains. All were fearful of making any change. Three who were willing to carry Polly's suggestion to their menfolk, came back to tell her the men were satisfied with present arrangements and knew the party they were traveling with would not take anybody else.

That evening, while Colin Brush was milking, Polly told him about what she had been doing.

"Keep at it!" he urged with a cautious backward glance. "I've asked around some too. We'll find some that want to join up, Polly. We'll both keep at it, but don't let *her* know—her and Daughter!"

The girl kept at the task she had set herself, but the days that followed were all like the first, except that as time passed she had to fight against disheartenment. Too she noticed things that were disturbing to her.

The grass came up slowly. Everyone was watching it grow. Near by it was grazed off as soon as the animals could nip it. The men would go into the prairie and return with tender green blades which they would compare and talk about in troubled groups.

The ever-growing camp became less orderly, as impatience and anxiety increased. At first there had been very little drinking, but day by day both drinking and gambling increased.

Neither general sanitary regulations nor temporary government was established, and many of the incoming trains scattered in disorder. Wagons everywhere were rummaged by their owners, and goods, clothing, and bedding of every kind and color lay spread on the ground or over the big covers of the schooners for a thorough drying whenever the sun shone.

All day long there was constant noise: loud talk, loud laughter, occasional hammering, and the braying of mules. Banjos, harmonicas, and guitars could be heard far into the night, often accompanied by raucous singing.

Most of the trains, though they were called companies, were loosely organized. Only in rare instances were there ties of joint ownership binding the members together. Each individual owned, not a share in a company, but a single wagon, or even a third or half interest in one. Each company was also made up, not of friends nor of members of the same church, not of men of the same occupation or cultural heritage or with a common outlook on life, but of strangely assorted persons of all ages and of every kind turned suddenly into adventurers.

Many of the men had already grown too impatient over the long delay to be mindful of the hardships and dangers ahead. A few were constantly withdrawing from the various waiting groups and forming new companies of four or five wagons, and striking out into the unknown.

Polly frequently saw Lieutenant Butler, for he seemed to be constantly about the camp. Several times a day she would see him talking to one group of men or another, but she did not know what his purpose was. Sometimes she met him, but he always held himself aloof. He was always courteous, but he rarely paused for more than two or three words with her. However on the afternoon of the ninth of May she saw him ride out of his way to meet her.

"I suppose tomorrow you'll be off again, you and the Brushes," he said.

"Yes," she answered.

"Yes!" he repeated sharply. "Thousands are saying that after tomorrow there'll be no chance of a shortage of grass.

So tomorrow's the day. We're starting, too, and we'll have lots of company. Nothing has been organized, though something very important might have been done here in the fortnight or more we've been waiting. I suppose nothing will come of it."

His serious mood surprised Polly. "I thought all the trains had finished organizing," she said. "I know the Rock Island men have made their plans for the road. Eight of the forty-seven will stand guard every night until midnight, then eight others until four in the morning. Those will be relieved by eight who will take the cattle to feed and will guard them until breakfast."

"Will they? How many of the men in this camp will obey orders?" Butler asked. "Not many of ours will. We've already lost two wagons, and there are all kinds of rumblings of dissension." At that moment a game of cards in progress had caught his eye: four players sitting on the ground, with perhaps a dozen idlers looking on. He turned to the girl suddenly.

"Miss Kent," he said, "there'll be a meeting of captains and others this evening near Brush's wagon, 'The Wolverene.' Will you ask Mr. Brush to be there, please?"

He appeared so troubled that after he had gone, Polly sat thinking about him. She was afraid that the dissensions in his train were extremely serious.

Just as she was about to go to see a woman whose husband she and Colin had almost persuaded to join them, she was confronted by Murillo. He had managed to find her several times since their first ride together. She had enjoyed seeing him, but she did not want him with her now.

"Mr. Murillo . . ." she began a little nettled.

"Now, Polly!" he interrupted pleadingly, "call me Bill, and . . . it's friendlier! You call me Bill, and I'll drop back and wait whenever a woman looms up anywhere."

"But, Mr. Murillo," she answered. "I don't want you to wait!"

"Why?" he persisted, keeping close beside her and trying to look disconsolate. "A girl as beautiful, as fascinating as you ought not to object to a little attention."

Polly laughed and came to a halt. "If you could only see yourself!" she said. "*You* are the one that is beautiful! Your light felt beaver! Your fine duds! That wonderful white horse of yours! Don't you know that even a girl as fascinating as I am can't get any other woman's attention if you're waiting forty yards away? I am on a serious errand—good-by, Mr. Murillo!"

He reined in his mount and sat watching her, smiling, but with knitted brows.

The woman said that her husband had decided to stay in the train they were with and so Polly soon left her. She was out again early that evening, and a little later she returned dejectedly to her own wagon.

Nearly a hundred men stood a few steps away, many of them watching her unsaddle. Presently she saw Butler ride in among them.

"Well, how's prospects?" one of the group inquired.

"Just think what this encampment means," Butler answered without dismounting. "This migration is far beyond anyone's expectations. Instead of a few hundreds, there are many thousands. At Fort Leavenworth, there's an encampment like this one. There's another at Weston and one at Council Bluffs."

"We know all that!" someone objected. "What we want to know is how this camp is lining up on your proposition."

"Most of the trains are not interested," Butler answered. "About a third who've come to this meeting I've called are captains. That's enough to start, I should say, if we can get together."

"Not if we *can!*" an objector interposed, "if we *want* to!"

"If you don't want to, God help us!" Butler exclaimed. Polly leaned forward, eager not to miss a word. Lieutenant Butler was right—and the men were indifferent. "In and around St. Joe right now there are fifteen thousand men, possibly twenty thousand, waiting to start on toward California. And there's only one road for all of us to travel. One road from here to Fort Kearney, three hundred miles away. At Fort Kearney, thousands more from Council Bluffs will swing onto the same road—the one road for all of us from there on for many hundreds of miles. What will happen to that dirt road with all those thousands of wagons? How long will the grass alongside it feed all the teams?"

"It's for us to beat the Council Bluffers to Kearney and lead 'em a chase from there," one man shouted. "An' we've got no time to waste in palaver. We've got our train officered good. That's all we want."

"Your train will be merely a small part of a great army," Butler answered. "Not an army—no, an uncontrolled multitude

10

—racing across a vast stretch of country that none of us knows anything about. What good will it do your train to have good officers if the grass is all eaten off ahead of you?"

"Say!" one captain put in, "you're going by the geography map that's marked 'Great American Desert' everywhere from Canada all the way down south to Texas, and from here clean out to the Rockies. That *Great American Desert's* all bosh!"

"We know it is," Butler answered. "Captain Bonneville's expedition helped to wipe that desert off the map. And he found the road that our wagons are to travel. He proved that wagons can cross the Rockies. Now *our* problem is to get these tens of thousands of emigrants through with their animals and wagons. If we can get enough trains organized to help maintain some kind of law and order and to keep men scouting and reporting back all along the line, we'll get through, all of us. The important thing is for enough trains to organize for a few purposes that all can agree on."

"And, Lieutenant," came an interruption, "I suppose you'll be the general, and boss the hull lot of us."

Many in the crowd laughed, but Polly clenched her hands. Why couldn't they understand?

"You need a general, but I'm not looking for the job," Butler answered, quietly. "I'd like to see thousands of men who are headed for death and disaster saved. I want a body of mounted scouts formed to look over the ground ahead of this multitude and report back to a staff of captains.

"I want to see the staff of captains invested with authority and with the duty imposed on them, to send carefully gathered information back to those behind concerning water and grass, the presence of hostile Indians, or any especially bad conditions ahead."

"Go to it, Lieutenant!" someone shouted. "Scout and send back all the information you like. But you won't have far to send it to the old mule train from Quincy, I'm tellin' you!"

"Unless you captains get together and take upon yourselves the responsibilities I've suggested, a scouting party will not be of any use," Butler commented.

"We've got organization enough," a wagon master objected. "Our train's goin' to California, and it ain't goin' under orders from nobody. We'll travel an' feed an' water where we like."

Others expressed approval of this. "That's talkin'!" one shouted.

"Time the rest git thar, we'll be loaded with gold!" another contributed.

"If you'd had any army experience, you'd know you haven't enough organization." Butler spoke earnestly. "Not even enough to keep discipline in your own trains. Not any of you."

"That's getting personal," someone interposed.

"It is personal!" Butler retorted. "It's something that comes right down to the members of your own companies. Strange things happen to the morale of men cut off from all the associations and restraints they've been accustomed to."

"Think you're talkin' in a church, Brother?"

Many laughed at this sally, but Butler kept his temper. "I'm thinking," he said, "that a banding together of many trains in this way that I'm urging will help you captains to

keep discipline among your own men. It will help to hold in
check thousands who, in the face of hardship or peril, with
no one in any kind of authority over them, may lose their
heads in unaccountable ways, and many of them their lives."

"What's to be scairt of but Indians?" someone asked.

"Many things," Butler answered. "We may find millions of
buffalo feeding on the plains. Millions in a single herd eating
off the grass we need for our teams. The great droves come
slowly north with the spring grass. This is a late season, very
late, as we all know, and we who get started first may pass
ahead of them.

"On the other hand, we may not. Besides, thousands of
emigrants will be coming on after us. And the buffalo means
more than a scarcity of grass. When a million buffaloes stampede
and are headed for a train, the only safety for it is to draw the
wagons in a circle, make a strong, closed corral, and get the
men and the mules and cattle inside.

"To do that right and in the least possible time, takes practice, otherwise emigrants and animals in the path of a running
herd will be swallowed up by it and trampled or carried off."

"Well, that's a good warning," one of the captains con-
ceded. "But we can handle our own trains and get to do it
fast."

"Anything that makes for discipline over the long stretch
we all have to travel will be a safeguard for every one of us.
How many of you will help to organize now for systematic
scouting the whole way and for some kind of law and order?"
Butler asked.

The silence that followed his inquiry was broken by the laughter of two or three, then by the laughter of many. Polly saw that a gnarled, bandy-legged little man who bore a big bundle on his back and held a dejected, heavily burdened gray donkey by a halter rope had caught the crowd's attention.

Behind the donkey, Bill Murillo sat on his superb white stallion. A floppy old hat had replaced his fine beaver, his flannel shirt was glaringly red, his shapeless blue jeans were tucked into mud-caked boots. He was looking at Polly, who, with Mrs. Brush and Ann, had been listening to the talk. Polly, however, did not let him see that she had noticed him.

"Hey, peddler! Show us your goods!" one of the men shouted. No answer came, and the man started threateningly toward the bent figure. "Open your pack!" he ordered. "Hear what I tell you?"

Instantly the white stallion moved forward, and Murillo leaned down.

"Let this man alone!" he said in a chill tone to the baiter, "he's a friend of mine!" Sitting erect again in his saddle, he reined the horse back to where it had been the moment before. Just then he saw that Polly was looking at him, so he doffed the battered hat with as gallant a sweep as ever he had made with the fine beaver.

The peddler's bent figure straightened, and a grand red beard came into view. Sea-blue eyes twinkled at Murillo from under bushy brows, and out of the beard rolled a voice with enough volume for a man twice its owner's size.

"The name is MacTaggart," he roared. "Jamie MacTaggart." Laughter rippled through the crowd, but the peddler was undisturbed. "If we wadna hae a throughither journey," he said, "let all gie heed to Mr. Butler."

"Thank you!" Butler answered.

That was the end of the meeting, but a few of the men hurled back comments as they were leaving:

"You mean good, Lieutenant, but there's nothing to it."

"If you get any information, send 'er up ahead to us!"

One shouted, "Aw, what's to worry about?"

"Those of us who are alive will know the answer to that by the end of the summer," Butler returned calmly.

"Mercy, Lieutenant Butler!" cried Mrs. Brush. "You don't think it'll be as bad as that, do you?"

"Not for you women," Butler answered dismounting and looking at Brush. "You're a steadying influence."

"But . . . but the buffaloes!" Eusebia gasped.

"The season's late, and we're ready to start. We may not even see any," Butler assured her. "But I'm surprised you didn't support me," he turned to say to Colin. "I've seen hundreds of wagons with women in them here in camp. Their men could organize a party that would keep discipline and a constant watchfulness, because every man would be bound to that train by the strongest possible ties."

Polly understood now why she had seen Lieutenant Butler talking so often to groups of men in the camp.

"But the parties with a few women in them don't want any more," she said. "The men who have brought their wives along are not willing to break away from the trains they are already with. I've found that out."

"I didn't support you at the meeting because you were talking to captains of trains and to men in trains, while we have only a couple of wagons," Brush explained. "I think your plan would be a godsend."

"I'll join your scouting party, Lieutenant," Polly volunteered.

"I'll drive your ponies the whole way, so that you can," Ann offered stoutly.

"There would have to be many scouts." Butler looked at Polly and smiled. "I'm afraid there'd be only two of us."

"Three!" Murillo said.

Butler merely glanced toward the speaker, then when he held Polly's eyes again, he added, "But if I thought I could form a scouting party that would accomplish anything, I'd pick you among the first."

For a moment the girl's tanned cheeks were flushed. But she was saved further embarrassment, for just then a wagon drawn by five oxen and one cow stopped behind Butler. A mere girl, with anxiously questioning eyes, looked out from under the mud-stained canvas hood at Mrs. Brush. The young man beside the cattle turned to Colin.

"We'd like to join up with you," he said. "We come from Pittsburgh. My wife, she's expecting a baby, and she wants to be near some women."

"But . . ." Brush stared at him.

"Waesucks!" MacTaggart muttered softly. "She's naught but a bairn herself!" With his brows knit and his eyes closed, he wagged his head from side to side as if in great pain. Then he started away hurriedly, leading his donkey.

"Why, we're moving out of camp tomorrow!" Brush finally said. "At daylight tomorrow!"

"We'll be ready." The young man, who hardly seemed more than a big, powerful boy still in his teens, looked back at the anxious face in the wagon. "Abbie wants to be along of somebody that knows. My name's Will—William Brazos."

"You'd better stay with your own train," Brush urged.

"The men voted to keep to men," young Brazos told him. "And all three o' the wagons we calc'lated to stay with, on account they had women, pulled out a while back when I wa'n't around."

"Sebie," Brush said helplessly, "did you hear that?"

"I heard," Eusebia answered, and made an effort to smile at the girl. "All right!" she said, nodding to her, "light down. We might as well be getting acquainted."

X

SEBIE BUYS A BASKET

THE road from the great camp on the bluff across from St. Joseph continued up the river fifteen miles and then swung west at the "Mission," which was pointed out as the only house west of the Missouri between Leavenworth and Canada. From there it followed the Nemeha for a time, crossed a branch of the Little Blue, and stretched away endlessly over a high, dry prairie to the new Fort Kearney on the Platte.

Wagons lumbered hurriedly, jolting over the three hundred miles toward the fort, and in all that distance the only Indians Polly saw were in the valley of the Nemeha. Two very old squaws, barely alive, near a deserted village, and a hundred or more dead hanging in the low, crooked trees of an Indian cemetery where, among weapons, kettles, and other once treasured possessions, they lay wrapped in rotting blankets

139

on burial stagings of two-inch poles held together by withes
of bark—that was all.

The girl rode aside to where the two withered, rheumy-eyed
hags were squatting in the sun. When she was a child, she had
heard her father tell of the Indian custom of leaving the very
old squaws behind, together with a few scraps of food, to die
alone when they could no longer keep up with a roving band.

Dismounting at once, she took from her saddle horn a shot
pouch, from which she poured half of the parched corn she was
carrying for her noonday meal into the lap of each of the two
pitiful creatures.

Polly scouted on ahead each day, always traveling alongside
the wagons, for the way was lined with them in both directions.
The road itself had been left clearly marked, in places deeply
rutted, by the wheels of several hundred home seekers who had
set out by this route for Oregon in May of the previous year.

The gold seekers, however, eager to gain the lead in this race
for fortune, could not keep to the one-track trail across the
wilds, but they drove in parallel columns, often three or four
wagons abreast, cutting new ruts in the yielding sod.

Polly remembered her father had told her that for two or
three hundred miles this country west of the Missouri was one
of sudden, violent storms where the swales filled quickly. At
her insistence, the Brush party, which consisted now of two
men and four women, camped each night on high ground of
her choosing.

The girls slept in Polly's wagon, which always had a place
in camp close to the big Brush schooner. Mornings and evenings

provided routine tasks for all. Ann began by setting up the
little stove which her mother still insisted on carrying, instead
of letting Polly have it. Colin milked and kept everything in
condition for travel. Polly looked after her own chores, while
Eusebia made biscuits and fried bacon.

At night, Polly always tied her two buckskin ponies by side-
lining them; that is, by roping the hind foot and the forefoot
of each on the same side, with eighteen inches of play between.
To one of the buckskins as a pivot, she securely tied her saddle
mare foot free, so that it could run around, cavort, and give
alarm in case of danger.

Sometimes the camp sites were a mile or more off the road,
and Brush and Brazos would grumble because a few of the
wagons in the rear of the endless procession would slip past
in the early dawn before they could regain their places in the
line. In addition, they grumbled because they did not see a
cloud nor a drop of rain between the tenth of May, when they
and the Rock Island train left the bluff across from St. Joseph,
and their arrival within sight of Fort Kearney on the thirtieth.

Even in this region, many of the emigrants were finding travel
difficult. The road was nearly always firm and there was grass,
though it was still short for grazing. The far-flung green of
the prairie was sprinkled with pools, and in every pool, though
it might have no outlet, and in all the small streams as well,
the water was good to drink.

But over a wide stretch of country each way from the road,
Polly could come upon no game, except an occasional antelope
flying like the wind. There were no prairie chicken and no

quail, and not even any buffalo. Several of the trains sent mounted men to hunt far beyond the wagons. They reported that the late spring had held the great herds far to the south, and that all the other wild things, frightened by the coming of the wagons, had fled beyond reach.

When the grazing was better, some of the trains covered twenty miles a day for a week before they reached Fort Kearney. All the men and Polly, as well as Mrs. Brush, Ann, and most of the other women emigrants, walked much of the time to lighten the loads; and they were all beginning to show the wear of continuous travel. Many of the men disregarded orders, shirked their routine tasks of the camp, and were quarrelsome.

On the afternoon of May thirtieth, the Rock Island train arrived at the edge of the bluffs. Fifteen miles away, the long strip of cottonwoods skirting the Platte could be seen. Barnett, the wagon master, had driven ahead with the spring wagon to select a camping ground. When the train halted five miles beyond the bluff and formed a corral for the night, there was not a cloud in the sky. The cattle were turned out on the scant grass with eight guards to watch them.

In ten minutes came sudden darkness, though it was barely past sunset, and low black clouds streamed over the prairie with incredible speed. The men all ran to help the herders, but when the cattle were within a hundred yards of the wagons, the storm struck them head-on. It turned them around and sent them running madly before the wind, the lightning that came in blinding flashes ripping the clouds close over their heads, and the thunder crashing all about them with terrifying violence.

Before the cattle had run a mile, the thunder, lightning, and rain swept past and the wind quieted. The oxen stopped and some began to graze, but many of them stood stock still in rain water six inches deep, on what otherwise appeared to be level ground.

By nine that evening, after the cattle had all been driven in and tied, the men not on guard went to sleep in the wagons. In the morning it was found that those on guard also had gone to bed and that the wagons were standing in freezing cold water more than two feet deep. The vast, steadily ascending plain over which the rain had swept was still pouring its storm flood down to the streams and into the swales of this lower region.

The men, as they yoked their oxen under a cloudless sky soon after dawn, waded wrathfully in the rising water. Each wagon group, refusing to wait for the others, started for the river without any breakfast.

The members of the Brush party saw a number of other trains nearly drowned out, but at their own high camp they drank their coffee at daylight, ate their fried bacon and cold biscuits, and went through their usual morning routine without discomfort.

After sunup they could see two thousand wagons or more off near the fort, where a stream of emigrants from Council Bluffs was pouring into the one road which all must travel into the west. Polly was certain that Colin's oxen were among the first five hundred yoked teams to reach the Platte, but she could see three or four times as many mule teams.

At the fort, travelers who could write, left letters to be sent back to the land of towns, villages, and homes when opportunity offered. Polly had written only to Mother Theodora Guerin of Saint-Mary-of-the-Woods, but she knew that more than one good sister would be anxiously awaiting that letter. Eusebia and Ann each had a handful of bulky envelopes ready for relatives and friends. From a diary he was keeping, Brush tore a number of pages to be mailed to his mother in Detroit.

When Polly arrived at the fort, she heard an emigrant say to the sentry at the gate, "I want to see Captain Ruff. Is that him coming?"

The sentry shook his head. At the moment, a mild-looking army captain in his early fifties, with a sturdy body and pleasant black eyes, rode briskly out of the frontier post on a well-groomed bay. With him were half a dozen men not in uniform.

After they had passed, Polly went in to leave the letters and stayed for a time to look around. On her way out, she heard the emigrant who had been questioning the sentry call to him again, "Why didn't you tell me that was Captain Bonneville?"

The girl stopped when she heard that name.

"You asked for Captain Ruff," the sentry answered.

"I wanted to see whoever was in command of the post!" returned the emigrant angrily.

"Did he say Captain Bonneville?" Polly interrupted.

"Yes, Miss," the guard answered. "Captain Bonneville took over command here from Captain Ruff yesterday."

"Captain Benjamin Bonneville?" Polly inquired eagerly.

The young soldier smiled at her and nodded.

"Oh, I wanted to see him!" she cried in disappointment.

"I know why," the soldier said. "Because you've read that book Washington Irving wrote about him and his explorations in the Rockies."

"I hadn't any idea he was here!" the girl exclaimed. "I want to speak to him! Where is he?"

"He headed east, and must be out of sight by now," the guard told her.

"How soon is he coming back?"

"No telling. All I know is he's to have a powwow with some Indian chiefs before long. He may be back in a couple of days." As long as she could remember, she had been eager to meet Captain Bonneville, but she could not wait to see him now. So she left a note telling him this, and of the time and place of her father's death. When she returned to the road, which held to the south side of the Platte after passing the army post, she was a long distance ahead of Colin's wagon, and she did not turn back.

A few miles beyond, in a great swale that had to be crossed, she saw hundreds of mules stuck in the mud. When they tried to pull their heavy loads, their feet and legs broke through the light sod and down the floundering animals would go. Although the place was not flooded, getting them up was difficult.

These mules belonged to a train from Pittsburgh, the members of which had spent the entire morning trying to get their sixty wagons across the swale without throwing anything away. Polly watched the men as they at last decided to hitch all their teams to thirty of the wagons and hurry on, leaving the other thirty behind.

The train captain hailed the crowd that had gathered and held a mock auction, offering all the abandoned, mired wagons for sale. Jamie MacTaggart gravely bid them in for a dollar, and he refused to pay until he received a bill of sale.

It was afternoon before Brush reached the place where he could see the swale, where some of the doubled-up mule teams were still floundering. At once he turned off the road to a piece of high ground and halted.

"Before we go down there, let's grease up again!" he called to Brazos. "That's a bad bit of ground, even for oxen." When he saw Polly returning, he shouted to her, "Think of those fellows having to waste a whole day coming back for their schooners! They're in for it!"

"They're not coming back," she answered.

"You wait and see!"

"No," she said, "they've sold the wagons."

"Sold them? Who to?" Brush was jacking up his wagon.

"The little red-bearded man with the gray donkey. Thirty wagons and all the scads of things that are in them—all for a dollar."

"Good lawsy!" cried Brush. "Does he think a party without wagons will ever come along this far from anywhere to buy them? He's crazy!"

"Sh!" Polly warned. "He's coming now."

Brazos, busy greasing an axle, was smiling. "How many o' them prairie schooners does 'e think him an' that long-eared beast o' hisn ought to haul to one load?" he asked. "All of 'em?"

"Miss Kent!" MacTaggart shouted as he hurried toward her, "Wad you ken a mule or an ox I could purchase?" The Scotchman had left his own bundle behind and was tugging hard to speed the donkey which still carried its pack.

"I hear you've got one bargain already," Brush called, before the girl could answer. "Or would that be a Scotch joke?"

"Wi' a dollar out of pocket?" Jamie smiled as he wiped the perspiration off his forehead with a grimy handkerchief. "It wad be a bargain, Mr. Brush, if Wee Jock here could be three instead of one. I hae goods to transport."

"How much you pay for one o' my teams?" Brazos asked, and winked at Colin.

William Brazos was very young, and a little slow; but he had a great store of strength in his heavy shoulders and huge, sure hands.

MacTaggart did not answer. He did not hear, for he was staring at a small band of Indians, all mounted. The first he had ever seen. Fifty or more of them were riding close together, and behind them a few bucks drove two or three hundred shaggy ponies. All had crossed the road in a draw, down which a brooklet was flowing after the storm, and were headed toward the fort.

"Look!" MacTaggart cried. "What do you name the conveyances some of the horses hae hitched behind them?"

11

"Travois," Polly told him. "They are like shafts, with the back ends braced wide apart and dragging on the ground. The two poles that form the shafts have a strong basket-like hammock of buffalo hide swung between them in which the squaws carry most everything."

"You ken the wild folk?" he asked quickly.

"My father often told me about them," Polly answered.

"Travois!" MacTaggart shouted. "Stop, travois! Come upby!" He waved his arms. "A word wi' you!"

"Oh, don't call them up here!" Mrs. Brush cried. "You'll have us all killed! Ann, get near your father! Quick, child!"

All the wagons in the road had halted, and from them the emigrants were staring at the Indians, who had stopped and were watching MacTaggart. Brush and Brazos left their work and moved so that they could reach up for their rifles.

"Don't ever let an Indian see that you're afraid!" Polly warned them. "If they see you're not afraid, they'll not bother you. And look how many of us there are. We're like an army."

MacTaggart had turned to listen to her. He straightened, swelled out his chest, and shouted to the Indians, "Do you speak English?"

A squaw came toward him, her pony, with its heavily loaded travois, keeping close at her heels. A few other squaws followed her, then some bucks, and soon the whole band was approaching. The squaw in the lead, young and lighter of skin than the others, drew near to Jamie and stood waiting. "What do you want?" she asked him.

"Squaw lady," he said, "I ettle to niffer for three or four conveyances. Take me to the person that—'deed no!—let the person that has conveyances to sell come upby."

"You talk English? Father to me Boston man—fur comp'ny. Me talk English," the squaw answered loftily.

MacTaggart, taken aback, glanced at one of the emigrants, who had burst into laughter and said, speaking slowly and distinctly, "Three ponies—three travois—what price, lady?"

An old Indian chief came riding forward to be at the head of the band. Feathers adorned his head; fine garments of tanned skins splotched with brilliant colors for a ceremonial visit at the fort covered his body; and paint decorated his wrinkled old weather-beaten face. He looked toward the halted wagons along the road, from which a number of men were coming on a run with their rifles, and spoke to the young squaw.

"Pawnee!" she said. "No on warpath! Friend!" After speaking a few words to the chief, who merely grunted in reply, she cried, "No swap pony."

"Fifteen dollars!" Jamie offered. And after a long silence, "Twenty!"

The squaw looked at the chief, waiting for him to give answer, but he said nothing.

"No swap," she repeated.

The white men, as they hastened up, saw that there was no trouble and stood looking at the Indians, but remained on the alert, fearing treachery.

"Twenty-five! Thirty dollars!" MacTaggart bid on. "Three ponies—three travois—forty dollars! Forty-five! Fifty!" He shook his head in disgust, looked at the listening, watchful emigrants, and exclaimed, "A waff folk! They hae no sense of business!"

The old chief looked steadily, stonily at him without any change of expression.

Suddenly MacTaggart spoke directly to the chief. "English? Do *you* speak English?" The query brought no answer, but Jamie persisted. "Sprechen sie Deutsch? Parlez vous français?" He turned again to the white listeners, tapped his head sadly, and remarked, "He gets no gliff of sense from it."

The young squaw had begun to rummage in the load behind her pony. She lifted out a clean new basket and placed it carefully on the ground in front of Mrs. Brush.

"Me swap basket. You swap corn?" she asked.

"Why—why I'd like to." Eusebia spoke as if she were afraid even to answer.

"Corn what fill basket, you give?"

Eusebia looked at Colin. "It's the nicest basket I ever saw," she said. "Such a pretty shape. And it won't hold many ears of corn, Colin." She was forgetting her fears in her delight over the basket.

"What on earth could you do with it on this trip?" Brush exclaimed. "The wagon's full already!"

"But it's so pretty!" Eusebia pleaded. "And it don't weigh anything. I can stuff it full, so it won't waste any room."

Her husband looked at her as she stood staring down admiringly. The lines of fatigue which had settled in her face on this long trip had now vanished.

"Come now, you don't really want it," he said. "Do you?"
She nodded, and Brush crawled up under the wagon hood.

"Why, of course I do!" she cried happily, when she saw
what he was going to do.

In a few moments Brush tossed out a sack partly filled with
corn. At the sharp command of the Indian chief, several squaws
at once moved up. One of them spread a blanket on the ground,
and two others dumped most of the corn on it. Then they all
squatted silently about the blanket and began to shell the
corn. They did this expertly and very quickly and threw the
cobs away.

"O Colin!" Mrs. Brush gasped. "I didn't say I'd give shelled
corn!"

Her husband shook his head. "Don't start any trouble,
Sebie," he warned. "Let 'em have it their own way now that
you've got into it."

The young squaw filled the basket heaping full, emptied
the corn out of it onto another blanket, and turned the basket
upside down. In this position the part that was the stand
proved to be a receptacle, which she now proceeded to fill.
When the corn had been emptied from this bottom cavity of
the basket, the squaw reached for the lid, which was arched
on the under side and had a rim on the top. Whether right
side up or reversed, it would hold a surprising quantity of
shelled corn, and in both positions the squaw filled it heaping
full.

The men who were looking on began to laugh. For some
time, MacTaggart had been so absorbed in watching the affair

that his mouth was agape. When he regained his composure, he reached down and patted the young squaw's shoulder.

"I hae you richt now," he said. "A canny folk, the Indians. Swap. That's the word for it. Swap." He hurried to his donkey, let down his pack, and opened it. "Bide until I prig wi' you!" he called.

When he came back, he had a coil of open-end brass thimbles. To show the different sizes, they had been strung on a heavy strand of leather with two large ends meeting, then two small ends, so that no thimble could be hidden by slipping inside another.

"Swap!" he cried. "What hae you to say to these?" He held up the thimbles and dangled them. "Come upby, squaw ladies! Look now! Made to endure a lifetime! And more than a plenty for everyone!"

He began to fumble with the knotted cord, trying to untie it. Although the squaws showed interest, none came any nearer. They looked at the chief, and the chief looked at the thimbles with half-closed eyes. Suddenly he spoke in a gruff voice to the squaw. The young squaw looked at MacTaggart. "Him swap," she said. "Five pony. Five travois."

Jamie's mouth dropped open. He shut it, swallowing twice before he could find his voice. "Ten they are worth," he said. "But they go for six." He held up six fingers.

The Indians stood silent, their faces expressionless, except the chief's, whose wide-open eyes gleamed a menace. MacTaggart, looking into those eyes, decided quickly, "Sold! Five ponies—five travois!"

The chief immediately rode up, reached down for the string of thimbles, and hung them proudly around his neck, after which he gave several quick orders.

"A necklace!" gasped the Scot. "Am I gone gowkit?"

In a very few minutes five ponies, each dragging a travois from which the load had been removed, were led up to him by several squaws. As soon as he had roped the ponies to keep them from following the band, the Indians went on their way to the fort.

"Stop!" MacTaggart shouted.

The Indians paused.

"Now I will swap thirty wagons! Look! Off yon in the bog! Thirty wagons, full loaded! Many barrels of sugar! Many barrels of flour! Bags of coffee! Chests of fine tea! Hams! Bacons! Fifteen ponies, fifteen travois. Take all! Except the men's clothing! That I keep!"

The chief turned, then went on his way, the whole band following.

"Ten ponies!" shouted MacTaggart after him. "Eight! Five! Three! One pony!"

Not an Indian turned his head. The armed emigrants gathered about began to laugh.

"He knows what he wants, that fella!" one of them cried out, pointing to the chief.

MacTaggart smiled. "Necklace!" he whispered. "Five ponies! Five travois!"

XI

POLLY WANTED THE BLACK WOLF

BEYOND the swale, the Pittsburgh train left panic in its
wake. Reduced to thirty wagons, each drawn by twice
the usual number of mules, it traveled so fast that the men
it passed saw themselves falling hopelessly behind, and set up
the cry: "Lighten the loads! The faster we go, the less we'll
have to carry!"

In some of the mule trains, there were quarrels and fights
over what should be done. Presently someone began to toss
supplies out of a wagon while it still kept to the road. This
example was promptly followed by others.

One train halted long enough to double up some of its teams,
and then went on, leaving several wagons. Other trains did the
same. Men who had spent months at home deciding just how
much of every kind of goods they must have to reach the

154

journey's end in safety, who had freighted their precious loads
hundreds of miles at heavy cost, now began to throw goods
and supplies away. This reckless craze for haste lasted nearly
a week, and left the roadsides littered for miles with discarded possessions of all kinds.

A ton more or a ton less, however, would make little difference in the plodding gait of oxen, consequently few men with
ox teams cut down their loads. Many of them feared that
they would be out of the race after they left the swale beyond
Fort Kearney, though some of them traveled twelve miles
the first afternoon.

"Don't they know," Polly bemoaned in camp that first
evening, "that we've no more miry road ahead for over a
month? Don't they know anything about what's ahead of
them?"

"How would they?" Brazos asked, from beside the cow he
was milking.

Polly, whose task it was to herd all the animals out to graze,
stood waiting for the men to finish milking the cows. She saw
Abbie Brazos stooping wearily over a campfire. This new
member of the party was always shy with Polly and Ann,
and they with her. She was nearer Ann's age than Polly's,
but she seemed far removed from the world of either. It was
only to Mrs. Brush that Abbie came, with a trust the good
woman found frightening.

Polly, looking across at the stooping figure, felt her anger
blaze at the man who could bring this young wife on such a
journey, with no knowledge of what lay ahead of them. But

she was schooling herself to hide her feelings and she merely said, "I suppose they wouldn't."

"Hardly more than four quarts," Brush complained, setting down his pail for Ann to care for. "At this rate, Kate'll be dry in another week, and May the week after."

Eusebia, who insisted on getting Polly's morning and evening meals along with her own, so as to give the girl additional time for scouting, stepped over and looked into the pail, but made no comment. She had already heard that the children among the emigrants were ill of a fever caused by drinking the milk from cows that were helping to haul the wagons.

"Ann," Polly said, "in the six hundred miles or more that we're to follow the Platte from here to Fort Laramie, there'll be only two rivers and one small creek to cross. So I'll not need to traipse back to help you at the fordings; and I'll have time to hunt in the hills we're coming to."

"Don't you dare do that!" cried Mrs. Brush.

"We have to have fresh meat," the girl answered. "We've gone so long without it."

Polly was ready to leave camp next morning before the oxen were yoked, and she did not let the others keep her long, for she was eager to be off. Bill Murillo, after leaving the encampment west of St. Joseph, had ridden with her frequently, too frequently she thought. There was a sparkling gaiety about him to which something in herself responded, but she had caught herself up at times—wondering. Only the day before she had seen a Rock Island man nudge another, and had heard him say:

"What'll you bet Murillo fixes up a partnership with Miss Terry Hut before we get across?"

" 'Taint long till Bill gets 'em eatin' out o' his hand," she heard the other one answer.

On this day Polly rode fast to keep Murillo from overtaking her. Until nearly noon she wore her sunbonnet, then she let it hang down her back by the strings because its closeness grew bothersome. When she had gone as far as the oxen could travel in a day, she struck south across the prairie.

In the first mile, she passed a number of wagons, the teams unhitched and feeding under armed guard. She passed a drove of four or five hundred mules out beyond the bluffs, which were more than five miles from the road, and the grass there was the best Polly had seen.

She knew that some of the larger trains were traveling fast at night when the road was clear. They camped in the daytime, because they could then take their animals far out to feed safely. The mules of the last party of these day campers that Polly passed nearly filled two little sunken meadows, but she did not see them until she was very close to them. The meadows were like potholes, each with a level floor of three or four acres covered with much better grass than any growing on the higher ground.

The part of the prairie Polly now came to seemed to be full of these potholes, one just like another, all rimmed in and hidden from view from anyone even a short distance away. Their lush green was dotted with buffalo skulls and bones bleached perfectly white.

The emigrants were all far behind the girl. Five or six miles away were the endless lines of trains sending up their low-hanging drift of dust. When she looked back, she could hardly tell whether the wagons were moving or standing still. If they were moving, they were certainly moving noiselessly.

Ahead, the living green of the prairie stretched on and on as far as she could see, swell rising above swell. Close around her were wild flowers of almost every hue, most of them flowers she had never seen before. She smiled as she tried to recall whether her father had ever mentioned them. She wondered if in all his travels he had ever been interested in the wild flowers or had ever even noticed them.

Polly rode along watching for game, and had thought there was none in the whole plain until an antelope sped up out of one of the potholes and was gone before she could take aim. She dismounted and, leading her saddle mare, went from one sunken meadow to another. When she drew near one, she dropped the bridle rein on the ground and let the pony graze while she crept to the rim and looked down, then she went back and led the pony again. All morning she hunted and crept up to dozens of potholes but found no game.

At noon she ate her parched corn, letting the mare graze her fill, then went on hunting. She was far out on the plain, and had hunted as long as she dared, when she crept up to one of the sunken meadows, looked over the rim, and nearly dropped her rifle. Startled she drew back trembling, for down in the meadow she had seen a pack of wolves. All but one seemed to be sitting still in a silent ring around the body of a dead buffalo—and a big gray wolf that was tearing at the flesh of the fresh kill. She knew the wolves in the circle were waiting their turn, and that none would dare dispute the right of the leader of the pack to pick and choose and finish his feast alone.

Not a sound came up from the meadow. For an instant, Polly had been too scared even to think of running to her pony. When she began to think clearly, she peered over very cautiously again. There was no break in the circle, and it seemed to her that not a wolf except the big one had moved. The brisk cross wind did not carry her scent to them, nor bring theirs to Keiēta.

Holding her head low, Polly crept back and drew a deep breath. Listening intently, she looked to see how far away Keiēta was, and discovered the pony near and grazing quietly. The girl thought that possibly in five seconds after firing a shot she could be in the saddle, flying to safety.

On the far side of the waiting circle there was one black wolf which would make a fine pelt. Suddenly Polly wanted that black pelt. She drew herself back to the edge of the rim, lay there resting her rifle on the ground while she took aim, and pressed the trigger.

She was sure she was in her saddle in less than the five seconds she had allowed herself, and in a moment more the pony was running. It was not until the girl had reached a piece of high ground that she glanced back. Then she saw, far away, three or four wolves pass like swift shadows from one draw to another and then vanish. They had been running away from her.

Polly had been certain the shot would frighten and scatter the pack so that she could go back and get the black pelt— if her aim was good. But now she shrank from returning. Before she could do it, she had to steel herself and wait until her nerves had quieted. After a minute or two she did go back, riding very slowly and cautiously.

All the way, she could see that ring of wolves on their haunches—waiting. She could count them. Starting with the black fellow and counting left to a heap of bleached buffalo bones, there were six—five more from there to a weathered buffalo skull—eight more to complete the ring—and the gray one alone at the feast—twenty in all.

She stayed in the saddle until she could look down into every part of the pothole, now startlingly empty, except for one wolf, the black one, and Polly could see that her shot had killed it. At last she rode down and began to skin it, but she kept an arm through her bridle rein and her rifle close beside her.

Every few moments she would glance up to watch the rim of the pothole. She worked fast, and was very skilful with her skinning knife. She had begun to loosen the pelt and strip it away, when, on looking up, she saw, just for an instant, the disappearing head of an Indian.

Her knife dropped from her hand. She picked it up and put it into the sheath which hung at her belt. Then she caught up her gun, and in an instant was in the saddle again. This time she rode slowly. Over and over she kept repeating to herself, "If Indians see that you're not afraid, they'll not harm you."

Looking up, she saw the disappearing head of an Indian.

Her father had told her this, and she believed it, but still she knew that she was afraid. She rode out of the sunken meadow at a walk, and for some distance kept her pony at a walking gait. Then she looked around. She and her pony were alone in the prairie. There was not a sign of either wolf or Indian. When she was too far from the edge of the rim for a bullet to reach her, she set the mare into a lope and soon was riding fast.

The long lines of wagon trains, which she saw when she topped a swell, were still far away, but they gave her a profound sense of relief and security. As she rode on, she began to feel ashamed of herself. Of course the wolves would run away at this time of year when she fired at them. And she knew the Indians were not on the warpath; she was certain they were all too friendly to harm anyone. When she was quite near the wagons, she was almost sorry she had not stayed to get the black wolf's pelt, but she did not care to go back for it.

Late that afternoon, the Brushes found Polly waiting for them, but without any game. After two more days of hunting, she returned with the hindquarters of an antelope hanging from her saddle.

It was the season of long days, and when Murillo and Hedges walked over from their camp that evening, the light was still lingering.

"What?" Hedges cried. "Nobody grumbling here? We've nothing but a lot of soreheads now! And the train's breaking up."

"Who's left you?" Brush inquired.

"Frezzell, Barnett, Doctor Brackett and his partner, Dimmock."

"Your captain and your wagon master both?" Eusebia exclaimed. "Who've you got for officers?"

"Nobody yet."

Hedges dropped wearily to the ground beside Ann, who suddenly became self-conscious and kept her eyes turned away from him. The big freckles which the spring sun had dotted over her delicate skin, making her look more like a child than she really was, were lost now under a bright tan which was deepening day by day.

When Mrs. Brush looked at her daughter, she felt like weeping; for Ann's complexion, fair like her father's, had been Eusebia's pride, and she had guarded it as something precious. But Hedges saw no unattractive change. When he looked at Ann, his eyes were frankly admiring.

Murillo, clean shaven, but still wearing the rough, travel-worn clothes he had donned before leaving the Missouri River bluff, stood looking down at Polly. He was much more gay and carefree than the other emigrants. To him the journey was a mere adventure, rather than a desperate gamble. He had borne all the cost of outfitting three wagons, the *Phoebe Ann*, *La Belle Antoinette*, and *Pretty Nelly*, with the understanding that his partner in each should leave him free from the drudgery of travel.

Occasionally he walked beside a team, and also turned out to guard the cattle at night whenever his turn came. But for

12

him there was no bone-fagging toil and no worry over what his luck might be at the end of the journey.

His lightness of spirit was comforting to Mrs. Brush. Day after day, as one train passed another, she could hear 'men shout to those they were leaving behind, "Root hog, or die!"

This taunt became distressing to her. Sometimes she could hear, "Gold ahead! Good-by!"

Now and then the losers in the race at the moment would answer, "Go it, Boots! We'll catch you!" But they generally took the taunts in scowling silence.

Mrs. Brush knew that the men rarely visited the members of other trains at the end of the day. In this steadily plodding throng, she long had missed any spirit of neighborliness or helpfulness which could have lessened the stark monotony of constant travel. She had been disturbed, even frightened, at first, by the absence of friendly interest among so many advancing thousands.

The coming of both Murillo and Hedges was disturbing. They had come, these same two, on other evenings, and Ann, although sixteen, was to her only a child. But Eusebia was kindly.

"You should 'ave come earlier," she said. "We had such a good meal. Roast antelope."

"May I go hunting with you next time, Polly?" Murillo asked. "I watched everywhere for you the last three days."

Polly looked at him and seemed to be considering the question. There was a long pause before she answered, "I'm sorry, but I think I hunt better alone."

"Ouch!" Bill exclaimed, grinning at her, but the grin was fleeting.

"Next time, Polly, bring me a buffalo," Eusebia urged. "That's the one thing I want to try my hand at."

"I don't care to hunt buffalo," the girl answered, "nor wolves either." She sat very still, staring straight before her.

"I'm beginning to think all this talk about great herds of buffalo covering the whole plains is a cock-and-bull tale," Brush said. "Anybody seen a single hide on the hoof?"

"Several hunters have sighted a few," Hedges answered. "But the big herds haven't got this far north. We're a week or ten days ahead of them."

"Listen!" Mrs. Brush interrupted. "You bring me a piece of good buffalo meat; then come over and I'll feed you sour-milk biscuits."

"We'll do that!" Murillo answered promptly, and he looked toward Polly to see if she would welcome his coming.

Just then Lieutenant Butler rode up and dismounted. "Our train hasn't overtaken you yet," he said, after a few words of greeting. "But we relayed across that swale and brought our wagons all through."

"Oxen have their good points after all," Brush answered, "even if they are slow."

"I was just telling 'em Polly shot an antelope," Eusebia informed the Lieutenant. "Too bad you didn't come in time to have some."

Butler looked at Polly intently. "The Indians steal oxen— prefer their meat to that of antelope—or mules," he said.

Polly, disconcerted by the steadiness of his gaze, looked away. "Well," Butler said calmly, "I may see you tomorrow."

Polly glanced up quickly in surprise at the shortness of his visit, and found him still looking at her. By a slight movement of his head, he signaled her to follow him, and started away without remounting.

The girl remained sitting cross-legged on the ground. She said good night to him with the others, and now she waited until he had gone a considerable distance. Then she called his name, as if she had suddenly thought of something she wished to say to him, got up quickly, and went to where he was standing.

"I didn't want to frighten Mrs. Brazos or the Brush women," he said in a low voice, "but you'd better keep a close watch tonight, and other nights, too, on your cattle."

"Sakes alive! We don't guard them at all," Polly told him. "We haven't enough people in our party for that. The cattle graze in the late evenings and for an hour or two in the early mornings. The rest of the night we keep them hobbled and tied close to the wagons."

"And you'd better not hunt far off the road," he warned.

"Because of the wolves, or because of the Indians lurking out in the potholes?"

"You know about the Indians?" Butler asked quickly. "How does that happen?"

"I saw one."

"When?"

"Three days ago. I'm not telling the Brushes."

"Tell me! I thought there weren't any Indians following us three days ago. I thought it was not till yesterday they began to. Tell me!"

"That's all; I just saw one and then came away."

"But I want you to tell me about it!"

He spoke as one in authority over her, but she was not displeased.

"Why, I was down in one of those potholes off south a ways where the country is full of them—of the little sunken meadows."

"I know!" he interrupted. "How far were you off the road?"

"It may have been six or seven miles."

"Too far! That's altogether too far for you to go alone!"

She thought it strange that he should be scolding her. "How far may I go after this, Mr. Butler?" she asked, laughing at him.

"And why did you go into a pothole where you couldn't see danger that might have been right near you?" he demanded sharply.

Polly was silent for a moment. "There was a dead buffalo down there," she said. "A big gray wolf was tearing at it. Other wolves, afraid of the big one, I suppose, were sitting around waiting. There were twenty in all. I'm not telling this to the Brushes."

"And you went down there?" he asked almost angrily.

"Not then." She laughed. "No, I stayed right where I was—lying on the slope—looking over the rim. To tell the truth, I was too scared to move."

Butler said nothing.

"But after a while I figured that in a few seconds I could get to the pony that was waiting behind me, jerk the rein up over her head, and be in the saddle on a dead run for the wagons."

"Well, then what?"

"I finally shot at one of the wolves—a black one—and didn't even wait to see what happened." She laughed again nervously. "Why, I was across the valley and nearly up the next ridge before it came to me that not a single wolf was following. Then I was ashamed of myself. But, just the same, I waited half an hour, I guess, before I went back."

"When did you see the Indian?"

"When I was trying to get the black wolf's pelt. It was like that basket Mrs. Brush got from the squaw: I didn't need that pelt, but I wanted it."

"Tell me the rest!"

"I happened to glance at the southern rim of the pothole and saw the head of an Indian disappearing. I didn't stay any longer, Lieutenant. And I didn't see the Indian again."

Butler stood considering this for a time. "Nearly all the hunters reported today that there are Indians off behind the low hills everywhere now watching the wagons," he said at last. "Entirely too many of them. They're up to something. That's why I stopped here. I'm passing the word along."

"You don't think they'll attack us, do you?" Polly said.

"No chance of that. They believe the whole white nation is moving to the setting sun, and they're afraid, awed by the vast numbers of us. Besides, we have no plows with us. If we were bringing the plows that have everywhere destroyed their hunting grounds, they might fight us, no matter how many we are. No, they'll not attack us, but they will steal our cattle."

"The Oregon settlers last year had plows. Didn't they get through?"

"Final word about them hasn't come back to Fort Kearney yet," Butler answered. "All that's known is that Indians did attack the Oregon train but were beaten off. We, with our picks and shovels, have nothing worse to fear than the stealing of our mules and oxen. But that would be calamity enough."

"I'll warn Colin Brush and Brazos," Polly offered.

"I've missed meeting you on the road lately," Butler said.

Polly stood silent.

"When do you hunt again?"

"Meat doesn't keep long this weather. In three days probably." She stood very still and waited.

He was frowning at her. "May I hunt with you?" he asked.

"Yes," she said, and turned away. In low voices they called good night to each other.

XII

A GRAVE FOR TWO

TWENTY oxen were stolen that night from a herd of more than five hundred belonging to a train of eighty wagons from Jackson County, Missouri. This was a matter of such importance that information about the loss spread quickly among neighboring camps. While Brush and Brazos were yoking up after breakfast, three of the Jackson County men appeared.

"Didn't see any stray steers, did you?" one of them asked.

"Not any," Brush answered. "Wasn't you warned last night about the Indians?"

"Warned? Sure we were," the man answered. "Not only warned, but we set double guard. An' most o' them that was sent out snuck back to their beds without any of us knowin' it and went to sleep."

"It was Indians took 'em," one of his companions stated. "But for a caution, we're lookin' around to make sure."

The three then went over to a small mule train that was beginning to move off a short distance away.

"Thunder and lightning!" Brush exclaimed. "Get that stuff back in the wagon!"

"I won't keep you but a minute, Colin!" Eusebia's voice came from under the canvas cover. "How would I know you'd be ready to start so soon?"

"She's only cleaning up a little and straightening a few things, Father," Ann said soothingly. "She'll soon be done."

"Must you always be digging around after dirt, like you was still back home?" Brush complained.

"It's like a house, a wagon is, when you live in it," Eusebia answered irritably. "It has to be kept clean."

"I'm all set, Mr. Brush!" Brazos called.

"So am I!" Colin answered. "But not my womenfolks! Get that stuff back in! Hurry!"

"Mother," Ann said in a whisper, "you'd better . . ."

"Hush!" Eusebia interrupted. "You begin handing in the things. What's a couple of minutes? We'd soon be living in a pigpen!"

Ann began to pass up bags and bundles, while her father stood by scowling, but without offering to help.

The near-by mule train was stringing out into line. Stealing the oxen had been the cause of greater activity than usual in most of the camps within a mile or more, and it seemed to Colin Brush that his was the only train not already on its way.

"Hurry!" he repeated. He swung about impatiently, and found himself face to face with two men standing a few feet from him and watching him intently.

"Good morning!" he said, in what could hardly be called a friendly tone. There was no answer to his greeting.

One of the men was very short and broad-shouldered. His right eye was turned outward, and the yellowish ball protruded, spreading wide the red and swollen lids. His companion was much taller than Brush, sharp-featured and sharp of glance. The taller man turned toward Brazos.

"Come over here a minute!" he called pleasantly. And when Brazos started toward him, the man looked at Polly, who was standing near her saddled pony. "You, too," he said. "Jest a minute."

As the girl left her pony and approached the little group, the short man backed off suddenly and swung up his rifle.

"You swine!" he snarled. "You will steal our oxen, will you! Put up your hands! All o' you!"

"Steal your oxen!" Brush cried indignantly.

"Up with 'em! I'll bore you!"

Brush, Brazos, and then Polly slowly raised their arms.

"You're makin' a mistake, Mister," Brazos cried, his face expressing dazed astonishment.

"That's enough out o' you!" snarled the man with the rifle. Then in a low voice he said, "Don't waste no more time, Jud!"

Mrs. Brush had repacked her wagon to her satisfaction and was making ready to climb down, unaware of what was happening. "There! That's something like!" she exclaimed, looking toward Abbie Brazos. Mrs. Brazos and Ann, too frightened to speak, were staring at the men. "That's been on my conscience . . ." Eusebia broke off suddenly and shrieked.

The tall stranger, his pistol drawn, strode toward her. "Come down out o' that wagon!" he ordered.

"Help!" Eusebia screamed. "Help! They're killing us!" She shouted toward the departing train.

The man with the pistol reached up, caught her by a wrist, and hauled her down so roughly that she fell. Brush and Brazos were standing with their backs turned, so they could not see this.

"Git over there with the rest!" the tall man ordered, as he jerked Eusebia to her feet. "All three o' you women! Git your hands up!"

Ann had sprung to her mother's side, fearing that she had been hurt. With this command, she raised her hands above her head as the other women had done, and went along with them.

"Stand right there!" the man with the rifle directed. "Don't a one of you move!"

Brush, Brazos, and the four women were lined up so that no one of them shielded another from the menace of the gun.

"Git the weapons out o' them wagons!" the short man growled.

"Wait a minute!" his companion answered. "A crowd's comin'!"

Polly, standing close beside her pony, which had followed her, could see a dozen or more men hurrying over from the mule train, which continued to move away.

"What's happening?" one of these men asked, as he and his companions came up.

"Jest gittin' back our four stole cattle. That lead yoke, an' the pair right behind 'em," the man with the pistol answered, with a jerk of his head toward Brush's team.

"*Your* cattle!" Brush cried. "That's a lie! I've drove 'em all the way from Detroit, Michigan!"

"They're not yours." Eusebia exclaimed. "That's our Broad and Star! Why, I never heard of such a thing!"

"Easy, Sebie!" Brush cautioned. "We can prove they're ours."

"When do you claim they was stole?" a bareheaded man, one of the newcomers, asked.

"Last night," the fellow, who had been addressed as Jud, answered after a moment of hesitation.

"You men camped right beside us last night. You saw we had those oxen then," Brush declared.

The bareheaded man conferred with others in his group. "Nobody in our crowd noticed your team," he then stated.

"That's too bad!" the fellow with the rifle interrupted. "If you'd seen *their* oxen, you'd know them four ain't theirn. Keep your hands up!"

"I suppose the Injuns stole theirn," Jud said. "That way, they had to have cattle or be left stranded, so they snuck off ourn that wa'nt guarded."

"It was their cattle that were stolen by Indians, I guess," Brush answered. "Anyway, these are ours. And it's easy proved. You men form a court right here. Get word to the

Rock Island train that'll be along here in a little while. We've traveled with 'em a month, and they know. 'Twon't take long to settle it."

The two men who claimed the cattle looked hard at each other for a moment, then the shorter one said, "That's right! Form a court! We'll try it out! An' afore we're done, we'll hang these folks, women an' all! There ain't no law out here; so we only meant to git our cattle back. But you start a court an' fetch the law, then we'll hang 'em!"

"Come on!" one of the mule train men cried in disgust. "We've no time to hunt up a lot of witnesses and hold a trial here."

"Leave 'em settle it themselves!" another said. "Where do we come wedgin' in?"

"Just a minute!" a companion of his interposed. "Hanged if I'll walk off leaving four women with their hands up, reaching for the sky!"

"Jest a minute yourself!" Jud exclaimed. "Wait right here where you be till I clean the guns out o' them wagons. We ain't no court to execute nobody, if they be thieves. We won't harm 'em none. An' we'll leave 'em right here. But we don't mean to give 'em guns to pick us off with while we're drivin' our oxen back." He turned and went to the wagons.

"Don't let him do it!" Eusebia pleaded. "They're our oxen! We can't go on or back without 'em!"

In a moment Jud returned with the rifles and belts and pistols belonging to Brush and Brazos. He laid these on the ground at a safe distance from their owners.

Most of the men who had answered Eusebia's call were hastening after their train. The one who had objected to leaving while the women's hands were raised, said, "Now you four put your hands down." He waited until the women had lowered their arms, then he and those of his party who had remained with him started away.

"Don't leave us!" Brush cried. "Give us a chance to get our witnesses!" but the men to whom he appealed paid no heed.

"You two jaspers keep yourn lifted!" the man with the rifle warned.

The taller of the two claimants of the oxen went to the team and took out four, yokes and all.

"Now you round up them other two hosses," his companion directed.

"You don't claim them, too, do you?" Polly asked.

The wall-eyed fellow grinned at her. "Listen, lady," he said, "ther' won't be no fast ridin' after we de-part. There ain't no law out here, only what I'm holdin' in my hands right now. An' we don't mean fer you to fetch no other. Take that saddle off!"

Polly's pony stood with head drooped as if asleep. The girl, while her arms had been raised, had moved slowly back against the mare so that Keiēta would not turn and show the rifle under the saddle flap next to the pad and on the side away from the men.

Polly now took hold of the rein close to the bit to keep the pony from moving, and went past her head to the side where the rifle was hidden.

"Mister!" she called sharply.

The wall-eyed man turned his head quickly, and as he did so, looked into the muzzle of Polly's gun.

"Drop it! Both of you lift your hands!" she ordered.

Neither man obeyed, but neither moved. Abbie Brazos screamed, crumpled, and sank to the ground unconscious.

Young Brazos, whose big, toil-hardened hands were awkwardly lifted above his head, glanced around and saw his wife. His mouth opened, and from it rumbled a sound like the growl of a huge dog. He leaped, and his hands came down swiftly on the rifle held by the short man, who was meanwhile watching Polly. He wrenched the gun away, and the next instant swung it upward.

The short fellow, seeing the menace of the weapon which Brazos was wielding as a club, tried to spring backward but brought up against one of the oxen passing close behind him. He bent sidewise in his effort to recover his balance and started to raise an arm defensively. Brazos, however, bashed the heavy rifle barrel against his temple, and he dropped. Then, as he was swinging the barrel up toward the tall man's chest, Brazos fired. Just as he was drawing the pistol he had put back in his belt when he began to unhook the oxen, the tall man, too, fell and lay outstretched on the ground.

Young Brazos, looking at the two at his feet, slowly lowered the rifle and let it fall. Going over to his wife, he picked her up and carried her to his wagon. There he lifted her to the seat and over it to the bed which was kept for her under the canvas cover.

"O God!" Eusebia prayed. "Help her!"

Colin Brush stood, staring wide-eyed at the now motionless pair who had come to steal his oxen. Polly, with one hand gripping the mane of her pony, let her rifle slip down until its butt rested on the ground.

Brazos backed out of his wagon, and without looking around, shouted at his team. Then taking up his goad, he struck one of the oxen. The cattle, moving up against their yokes, started slowly away.

"Wait! Wait!" Brush called. "We've got to do something about this!"

Brazos whirled and came back. With head thrust forward and eyes glaring, he stood in front of Brush.

"She don't know about it!" he said hoarsely. "I don't want she should— leastways not till after." He backed off, watching Colin with a steadiness of gaze that carried a threat. Then he turned, caught up with his cattle, and set to prodding them.

"Oh, what shall we do?" Eusebia cried.

Brush turned toward her slowly, his face ashen above his sun-bleached beard. In a moment he was staring toward the passing wagons—three endless streams of them, and countless men walking beside them in the early morning under a rising dust cloud that stretched along the apparently level valley of the Platte as far as he could see. Many of the men kept looking at him and the place where the shot had been fired as they passed, but they kept steadily on their way.

"No law here!" Brush muttered. "Nobody's business to see right done!" He looked down at the two that were still motionless. Then he saw his own pistol belt lying on the ground and put it on. He had not worn it in many days.

The man of the mule train who had insisted that the women be allowed to lower their hands came past the wagon now. He examined the two bodies hurriedly.

"Both dead," he declared. "You'd better pull out of here! Fast, too! Don't waste time!"

"And leave them like that?" Brush protested.

"I thought they were your oxen in the first place," the stranger answered. "And your friend who's driving ahead there has settled *their* claim. But before a lot of their friends show up, you'd better get your womenfolks to a better—a safer—place than this."

"Get into the wagon, Sebie," Brush called.

"Pull right out! Somebody camping here tonight, with plenty of time to spare for the job, can bury them." The stranger turned and walked briskly away.

Eusebia was so weak that Colin had to help her over the wheel.

"I'll drive, Ann," Polly said. "I guess I can."

"I couldn't," Ann whispered. "I think I'll ride with Mother."

Brush picked up his own rifle and the gun and pistol belt belonging to Brazos, and put them in the wagon. Then, as soon as he could rehitch the four oxen, he started.

Polly tied her saddle pony to the endgate of her wagon and kept close behind the Brushes. After she had gone nearly half a mile, she looked back for a moment. She could see two men from a passing train standing near the bodies. No other persons

12

were paying any attention. While she was looking, the two men turned and hurried off to catch up with the members of their own party.

An hour before noon, Lieutenant Butler, scouting ahead of the South Bend train, heard a woman moaning in a wagon at the roadside. A few steps off, young Brazos stood watching the passing trains, and Butler rode over to him.

"Something wrong?" he asked.

Brazos nodded in grief-stricken helplessness. "Brush's woman —could you get 'er, Mister?" he asked brokenly. "I've been waitin' here forever for 'em to come along. Abbie needs her bad, Mister!"

"Wait here," Butler answered. "They're not too far behind," and he turned his horse and rode back.

When the Brushes reached the place where Brazos was still waiting, Colin swung his oxen aside. He wheeled in beyond the other wagon and stood at the head of his team, undecided what to do, his goad in his hand.

Eusebia, who had been walking behind him, looked down at her calico dress, and suddenly began to shake the dust from it. "Unhitch!" she directed, taking authority. "There's the river! It's a good thing it's close! Get right down there before unhitching and build a fire. We'll need plenty of hot water." She hurried to the Brazos wagon.

Brush drove nearer to the river, and Brazos brought his team along.

"Unhitch!" Colin said, when the girls came up, wide-eyed and gravely silent. "That looks like good grass up the stream a little. You two girls run the stock up there and see they have a good feed. No telling how long we'll be here." He unhitched the Brazos oxen, too, and started them on to graze with the others.

The girls had gone, and a fire had been built in Polly's stove when Eusebia climbed down from under the hood that sheltered the moaning girl. Mrs. Brush saw that Colin had gone to the river for more water, so she went to young Brazos where he had thrown himself on the ground with his face on his arms.

"She needs a doctor," Eusebia told him, twisting her hands together in distress as she looked anxiously toward the passing emigrants. "Things ain't going right, and I don't know what to do. There's a doctor with the South Bend outfit—if only they'd come along soon! You best go back a ways, Mr. Brazos— see if you can meet Lieutenant Butler again. I think he went back to his outfit. Tell 'im I sent you."

Brazos had got to his feet. Without answering, he hurried away.

Butler, without waiting to be told what the need was, had ridden back to his own train. It was past noon when he reined his horse about and kept pace with the driver of one of the South Bend teams.

"Van," he said to him, "work just ahead for you. That Brazos girl I told you of across from St. Joe."

"A baby?" the driver asked.

"I suppose so. Anyway, she needs you."

"But what will I do?" Doctor Vanander exclaimed. "Look at me! I couldn't get myself clean for a job like that in a week!"

"Where's there another doctor who can?" Butler asked.

Vanander gave his whip to one of his two partners, stepped away from the road, and began to beat the dust from his clothes. He held out his grimy hands and turned them over slowly, scowling and muttering to himself. Then he hurried forward after his wagon and climbed into it. When he left it, he had on a clean shirt and new trousers and carried a physician's bag.

"Ride my horse," Butler said to him as he dismounted. "I'll stop there as I come along. You'll find their party off near the river, halted, of course."

Brazos, who had been watching the road, recognized Butler's horse and called to the rider.

"Are you Brazos?" the doctor called back cheerily. When he came near the halted wagons, he said, "You've got just what I need down yonder—plenty of hot water for me to scrub up with first thing. I've soap along."

At the sound of his voice, Mrs. Brush looked out from under the canvas cover. "Thank God!" she cried. "Don't wait, Doctor! Come!"

Doctor Vanander dismounted and answered Eusebia's summons at once. For a time there was ominous quiet in the Brazos wagon. But it was not long before he climbed out and helped Mrs. Brush down. She carried a bundle wrapped in white, a white skirt of Abbie's, and went toward her own wagon. The doctor walked slowly to the man who was lying face down, and caught him gently by the shoulder.

The girls forgot the cattle for the moment. Ann, with Polly close behind, ran to meet her mother.

"Is that the baby?" she asked. "I can't wait to see it!" She stopped short, as she looked at her mother's face.

"It's dead," Mrs. Brush said dully. "Such a pretty, sweet little girl." Suddenly the tears began to roll unheeded down her cheeks.

A new sound startled them.

"Abbie! Abbie!" A strong voice was calling. It seemed to silence suddenly the monotonous tread of teams and the rumble of wagons to which they had been accustomed for so long. Each time the name was called, the voice rose higher in anguish.

Mrs. Brush sank weakly to the ground with her burden. The two girls stared at each other with fright in their eyes. There was no need for Mrs. Brush to tell them that death had taken its toll twofold. Without looking up into their young faces, she said, "What happened this morning made everything go wrong. Poor girl! And her baby gone, too!"

She tried to think of something more to say that might lessen the tragedy for the two girls; but nothing came to her mind. Presently she folded back the white skirt, and the girls, kneeling close beside her, looked down at the tiny bit of delicate sculpture.

"I couldn't find the little clothes Abbie's ma helped 'er make. They're some place down in the load, but it's no use asking that boy to find 'em now. I reckon I can wrap a clean towel around it for burying."

"No!" Polly cried passionately. "No! I want her to have something fine! It's all she'll ever have in this world!" She got up quickly and went to her wagon. When she returned, she

held a piece of fine muslin, one end of which was deeply em-
broidered.

"You can't give that, Polly," Mrs. Brush told her. "You'll
never get anything more like it. It's the finest needlework I
ever . . . ever . . . "

"Mother!" Ann cried. "For that darling baby? Nothing is
too fine!"

"I can make more," Polly answered, "when my hands aren't
rough. And I have others—other pieces. One of them—the
sisters made me wait two years for just the right kind of floss
to come from France before they'd let me finish it."

Mrs. Brush was examining the exceedingly fine and closely
worked stitches. Then she held the muslin out in one hand at
arm's length. "This was meant for a baby dress," she decided
thoughtfully. "See, here's a bit of embroidery they made you do
at the top, and another here. They're for little puffs of sleeves."

"Is it?" Polly whispered. "No one ever told me."

"I guess they'd want you to give it, Polly," Mrs. Brush told
her.

Until she found her scissors, she carried the still bundle in
her arms. Then she laid the bundle down while she cut the
garment and showed the girls how to sew it up quickly with
their roughened fingers.

Late in the afternoon, Colin Brush came to Eusebia. "It's
no use asking any longer of the passing wagons," he said. "I
just can't get a minister. We'll have to lay them away without.
You see, Sebie, we ought to go on and camp close to the Rock
Island train tonight for safety."

A short distance back in the prairie he and Lieutenant Butler had dug a grave, and had lined it carefully with slender branches from the cottonwoods along the river.

Mrs. Brush went over to young Brazos, who was sitting with his head in his hands. He seemed not to hear when she told him that everything was ready. When she touched his arm, he lifted his head and looked at her with eyes like those of a wounded wild thing.

"I was aimin' to make 'er rich," he moaned thickly. "She was fitten fer nice things, Abbie was."

When the first spadeful of earth fell into the grave, he turned and walked unsteadily to his oxen which Brush had rehitched after they had grazed. By the time the grave had been filled, Brazos was lost in the never-ending stream of wagons.

XIII

CHOLERA AHEAD

THE valley of the Platte appeared to be level, but it rose steadily, mile after mile, toward the great divide of the Rockies which the gold seekers all expected to cross in mid-summer at South Pass. The bluffs between which the eastern end of the valley lay were now giving way to hills which rose higher and higher ahead, but no streams flowed down from those on the southern side of the river. The ascent, constant though imperceptible, was wearing on the animals, which were given no day of rest, even on the Sabbath. It was wearying as well to the travelers who either plodded on behind the wagons or walked beside the teams.

To every owner of a team, the finding of grass on which other teams had not grazed was becoming a problem of grave concern. By the end of the week, a hundred fifty miles

186

beyond Fort Kearney, a few emigrants here and there began to lose heart and turn homeward.

The men who had left Rock Island together all kept on toward the mountains, but some of them had withdrawn from the train. Only eleven of the seventeen wagons still remained in the party. In several of these there was brooding discontent.

Lester Lee and Freddie Dascomb, who had traded into a partnership, had been gay and busy, however, all the way from the fort. Taking turns, they had ransacked abandoned loads for food and other things they coveted, and had changed into new suits of clothes four or five times a day. At night, they had found wagons to burn in their campfires.

Polly, returning from her first hunt with Lieutenant Butler, saw what was left of the Rock Island train camped near her own little party, in which only herself and the Brushes now remained. They had not caught sight of Brazos again.

"We've got it!" Eusebia called to the girl. "Buffalo! They're coming right over to eat with us! We camped early on that account." She looked tired, but she continued to busy herself over the tiny stove.

A few steps away, meat was roasting at a big fire, and the evening air was filled with its appetizing odors. Bill Murillo stood near watching her.

"Hedges and I!" he called gleefully, as he hastened to meet Polly.

"And Lester Lee and Freddie Dascomb, too!" Eusebia called after him. "After all that's happened, I want young folks around. Freddie promised he'd bring his jew's-harp."

"Not Lester," Murillo answered. "He's pretty sick, Lester is."

Mrs. Brush straightened and looked toward the Rock Island corral. Against the glow of the late sunset, she could see men moving about their campfires ladling up food or squatting on the ground to eat.

The air was beginning to grow chill toward night, and sounds carried clearly from one camp to another. Someone in the train over there had got out a banjo, and a few young, lusty voices were accompanying it.

"What's the matter of Lester?" Eusebia asked.

"Don't know!" Murillo answered, as he took down a quarter of antelope from behind Polly's saddle. "Antelope? Pouf! Polly, you should have hunted with me today, instead of with your friend the lieutenant. Ran into a herd of six buffalo and shot two. Tonight everybody's feasting."

"It certainly smells good!" Polly exclaimed, in smiling anticipation. "I could eat your whole buffalo!"

"Me, too!" came from Brush, who was tinkering with his wagon. "It must be roasted enough, Sebie. Now that Polly's come, I'm going to call Daughter." He waved an arm and shouted, "Leave the cattle! Come on in, Honey!"

Hearing the call, Hedges and Freddie Dascomb came over. They and Murillo sniffed and then grinned at one another. Eusebia had set a pan of biscuits beside the stove to keep hot, and was now testing the roast.

"Can't you mix Gale up a batch of pancakes, Mrs. Brush, instead of these biscuits?" Murillo asked.

"Pancakes!" Hedges made a wry face. "I wish I never had to see another pancake! Since I left Rock Island, I've had enough pancakes to last a couple of lifetimes!"

"I never in all my born days saw anything take so long to cook as this meat does!" Eusebia spluttered in exasperation. "Yes, it must be done! It must be! We'll not wait any longer anyhow, or the biscuits won't be fit to eat."

She cut up the roast in generous hunks with a big sharp knife, and served it on the tin plates as fast as they were brought up to her. While the others were beginning their meal, she made a pan of gravy to be eaten with the biscuits.

"How is it?" she asked, aware of a long interval of silence.

Brush closed his eyes and swallowed. "It's done," he murmured.

Ann looked at Polly and almost choked. The others kept on chewing.

As Eusebia helped them to the gravy, she noticed the large pieces of roast still left on their plates. "Did I cook it tough?" she asked anxiously, as she set the gravy pan down.

Murillo did as Brush had done a few moments before—he shut his eyes and swallowed. "Nobody on earth could, Mrs. Brush!" he assured her. "No one could possibly *cook* this meat tough. It *was* tough. I've got good teeth, but I can't dent it. And, Polly, you should have heard me brag about it when I brought it to her!"

"How's the gravy?" Eusebia asked weakly.

"Oh, that? Fine!" Murillo exclaimed. "But the biscuits, say! They melt in your mouth!"

"Fine!" Brush growled. "A little of that gravy goes a mighty long ways, Sebie. It's the strongest gravy I ever tasted in my life."

"I'm sorry, Mrs. Brush!" Murillo said, seeing how disappointed and tired-looking she was.

Zenas Rose came across from the other wagons. "Did your buffalo meat cook up tender?" he asked.

"Tender as chicken," Murillo told him. "And the flavor! Zenas, it has character!"

"Well, I'll be hanged!" Rose exclaimed. "You can't get a hunk of ours chewed to save your life."

"Don't let 'em fool you, Mr. Rose," Eusebia said, dejectedly.

Rose looked at her a moment and grinned. "So that's how," he said. "One of our men says the old buffalo bulls go on ahead of the herds, sometimes in little stag parties of mebby a dozen or more. You must 'ave broke up a stag party, Bill."

The young folks laughed. Brush, who was watching his wife, could see that she felt her reputation as a cook had been saved by what Rose had said, so he laughed, too. At last even Eusebia joined in the fun.

Rose, who was laughing with the others, suddenly glanced around, then leaped to one side. A team of four oxen that were nearly spent was heading slowly toward him hitched to a wagon, but no one was driving.

"Hey! Whoa!" Rose shouted, and the oxen halted.

A figure that lay huddled on the seat up under the canvas hood raised to a sitting posture, proved to be a woman in a limp sunbonnet.

"Ain't there any driver for this team?" Rose asked.

"Only me," the woman answered dully.

There was a moment of silence; then all who had been laughing stood up and gazed at the woman.

"But, marm, you can't let your cattle just wander," Brush said, as he walked toward her slowly. "They'll run into something and wreck you."

The woman took off her sunbonnet and laid it on the seat beside her. Then she unfastened a rope which she had tied about her waist to keep her from falling off the seat as she slept. She may have been in her fifties, but her thin hair showed white in the light of the evening, and she looked withered and very old.

"They ain't wanderin'," she answered. "They're headin' home."

"Where are you from?" Brush asked.

"Well, I guess you better know," she declared. "I guess you better had. I come out o' the cholera camp six miles on ahead . . . mebby eight miles."

"Cholera camp!" Zenas Rose repeated. "What do you mean? You mean there's cholera up ahead?"

"It ketched Cal, my man, comin' last sundown but one— like it ketched the rest—sudden like. Next day it took 'im. I 'lowed it 'ud ketch me, too, so I waited. But I ain't never been lucky yet. So I give up waitin', an' started home."

She began to climb down, but changed her mind and from under the canvas cover pulled a long stick with which she could prod her lead team from the wagon seat.

"It's all I kin figger, Mister," she said wearily to Brush. "They're knowin' critters—oxen—an' headin' home keeps 'em goin'. Me sleepin' nights, I kin hunt grass daytimes, herd 'em, an' hold 'em fit."

"How do you know it was cholera?" Rose asked.

"Don't go look, Mister!" she answered in a dull monotone. "Take my tellin' fer it. How do I know? Folks layin' all around camp dyin' like flies. Cattle wanderin' off. Them that's left diggin' places fer the dead. They said it was cholera, Mister; an' I'd say it was. Ther' was a doctor come past, too, that said the same."

Reaching out her stick, she flicked it on the back of each ox, one after another, until her team started. The wheels creaked loudly on ungreased axles as her wagon moved past the group. None of those left behind spoke for a time.

"Freddie," Rose said at last, "go over and see how Lester is. I heard say he come down mighty sudden. I heard say he's mighty sick."

"You go," young Dascomb answered. "I wouldn't know if it was cholera or what it was. But you wouldn't know neither, Zenas. Can't we get a doctor for 'im?"

"What's it like?" Zenas asked. "Was you with him when he took down? What was it like? This is a mighty serious business, Freddie. We don't want cholera breaking out in our camp. Why don't you tell us?"

"First I noticed, he was thirsty, drunk a lot o' water," young Dascomb answered. "Then 'is stummick swelled up something turrible. Is that a sign?"

"By crackey!" Rose turned and looked toward the Rock Island corral, then strode to his own camp to tell the other members of the party. "I'll go and try to find a doctor," Murillo offered and started at once for his horse.

Several of the men to whom Rose had spoken hurried off to where the cattle were grazing. They came back very soon, driving the eight animals which belonged to the two boys and spanned them in.

"Haul your wagon a good ways off!" Rose shouted. "We can't have the whole camp take down with it!"

"Leave Freddie stay," one of the members of the party urged. "Mebby somebody'll double up and make room for 'im."

"If Lester goes, I go!" Freddie declared.

"Suit yourself," Rose told him. "But get going!"

"You two boys been rummaging into empty wagons all along the road from Fort Kearney," one of the men said. "No telling how much cholera they had in 'em."

Without answering, Freddie started his oxen and drove off.

XIV

THE LIGHTNING STRIKES

A DEEPLY interested young doctor questioned Lester, dosed him, but couldn't seem to help him.

"It's not cholera though," he said to Mrs. Brush, as he went past with Bill Murillo. "Too much water on top of too many raw dried peaches he found abandoned in a wagon back yonder. He munched peaches all afternoon, and they swelled up in him."

Lester was well enough to be righteously indignant next morning and to refuse to travel another mile with the Rock Island train. Pale and serious, his straggly hair uncombed and his cheeks showing thin through his scant blond beard, he was so appealing a figure that when he and Freddie asked Mrs. Brush just after sunrise if they could join her party, she accepted them without even consulting Colin and the girls.

194

Before noon, Brush turned off the road away from the river, as did all the trains ahead of him, to avoid a camp which seemed devoid of life, and Polly and the boys also made the detour.

From this time on, without knowing for many weeks how fortunate they were, they kept ahead of a scourge of cholera whose death toll among the tens of thousands in the long trail behind them soon became appalling.

Eight days after they passed the stricken camp, they forded the South Platte, which was about a half mile wide, but only six inches deep the greater part of the way. Where it was deepest, three feet of water flowed over quicksand in which an animal could easily sink out of sight if it did not move rapidly.

Brush and the boys, by placing wooden blocks on the holsters, raised all the wagon beds high enough to keep everything inside dry, and whipped the oxen safely across the river.

Polly, who was not allowed to help at this work, spent her time cutting large strips of hide from a buffalo bull that had just been killed by a party of Kentuckians who wanted only the meat.

Up the North Platte, the character of the country changed entirely. The road soon led to a great open plain where grass gave place to sagebrush and prickly pear, and where the water in the ponds was strongly alkaline. Within a few days the oxen and the ponies thinned down alarmingly and the cows went dry. Jack rabbits were the only game, but they furnished Polly and the Brushes many a good meal, some of which the boys shared.

14

Day after day, Colin watched the lines of wagons creeping over the plain ahead of him and behind him as far as he could see. He prodded his oxen constantly, not daring to lag behind in this race for gold which had now become a race for grass.

The animals stood up under their prodding surprisingly well, for though the days were hot, the nights were cool in this higher altitude, and nearly every afternoon brought a refreshing thunderstorm.

Beyond Court House Rock, the afternoon storm held off longer than usual, and when the party neared Chimney Rock, the sky became so black that Brush stopped his team in alarm.

"Polly!" he shouted. "Unhitch! You and the boys! Tie the stock to the wagon wheels and get under cover!"

Nearly all the other trains halted also. Everywhere men set to work in haste to get their animals securely tied. Eusebia barely had time to put out her bread pan and her camp kettles to catch water for cooking and drinking, when in an instant the day became as night over the whole plain. Jagged lightning pierced the darkness. Deafening thunder and a downpour that seemed like a cloudburst followed.

The canvas cover of the light wagon in which Polly and Ann had taken shelter was almost beaten in upon them, and they were wet by the spray that was driven through it. When the storm slackened and the thunder came rolling back from a distance, Polly pulled aside the seat guard and looked out. At that instant there came a blinding flash and close at hand a rending, shattering crash.

Polly thought she had been struck by lightning, but in the glare of another bolt, she saw Ann peering at her in terror, and she caught a stifling breath of sulphur. Then she heard Colin Brush calling, asking if they were hurt. Presently she saw him look into the wagon.

"I felt the shock!" Ann gasped, as she pushed back her sunbonnet to get a breath of air.

"Did you!" Polly asked, surprised to find that she could speak.

"We're all right now!" Brush assured them. "Don't be scared. It's growing light, so I guess it's over. But stay where you are, both of you, till I look around."

Though they remained under cover, the girls both looked out of the wagon. In a weird twilight, they could see drenched cattle and drenched wagons. One wagon was completely wrecked, the oxen that had been tied to its wheels lying dead about it. Toward the wreckage, from which a thin stream of white smoke was beginning to rise, dim figures were approaching.

"What wagon is it?" the girls heard someone up the line call anxiously.

"*The Phoebe Ann!*" Lester Lee's voice answered. "Fetch Bill Murillo! He's part owner!"

A stranger set to work quickly with his knife to cut the throats of the oxen and save the meat. When he had finished, he stepped back, wiping the blade on his shirt sleeve. "See here!" he cried out. "They don't bleed! Well, I never knew that before. Not even good for meat, after that lightning stroke."

"Hook up and haul off these near-by wagons while you can!" someone else shouted. "We're going to have a fire here! Get all these wagons away!"

"Climb out!" Brush called to the girls. "Get away from here as fast as you can!"

Gale Hedges suddenly appeared and helped for a few minutes. By the time Brush's and Polly's wagons had begun to move away from the wreckage, the thin stream of smoke had become a white column.

"That's one bad thing about these canvas covers," Brush complained. "They keep everything inside so dry that the lightning can set things afire right in a cloudburst." Once started, he did not stop with merely getting out of danger. In the west, directly ahead, the scudding cloud bank was leaving behind it a spreading view of distant mountains and a widening arc of blue sky in which the sun was shining, and all along the road, men were either rehitching or rounding up the oxen and mules that had broken loose in the height of the storm.

"Say, Mr. Brush!" Lester Lee shouted, as he came running forward. "There's something wrong with . . ."

"Keep quiet!" Colin whirled round in anger. "Come up here! Keep your mouth shut! Walk along here beside me quiet till we see what the trouble is!"

Lester, falling in beside Brush, whispered, "Four of our steers have gone crazy!"

"So have three of mine!" Brush answered. "Crazy acting— and eyes red as beets. But must you holler to the womenfolks about it?" He glanced back to where Eusebia and Ann were now hurrying to overtake him, after lingering to look at the, fire and the dead oxen.

"What is it?" Polly asked, as she caught up with the two men.

Neither one answered her, but she noticed that some of the oxen were shaking their heads and capering queerly.

"What is it?" she insisted. "Why are they acting like that?"

Lester whirled round and ran back to his own team, but in a few minutes he was up beside the girl again.

"Are any of yours acting like these?" she asked.

"Four," Lester answered. "Their eyes are red, too. What is it? The lightning?"

"I don't know," Polly said.

"We've got to stop!" Brush spoke softly. "Old Red there's going to lie down. Whoa!" He beckoned to Polly to come nearer. "Keep a tight tongue—that's a good girl," he whispered. "I don't know what the trouble is, but these steers'll be all right before long." Just then a rain-soaked man on horseback drew up beside the little group. Polly was surprised to see that he was Lieutenant Butler.

"They've been drinking alkali water," he said. Then he snapped out almost angrily, "Don't you know what to do about it?"

At the moment, his appearance was that of one whose nerves had got the better of him after days and nights of overwork and sleeplessness. He lifted a high-crowned, wide-brimmed Mexican hat hanging from his saddle horn and dismounted wearily.

"You've three sick cattle," he added. "Get a slab of fat bacon and a sharp knife."

Without waiting to ask any questions, Brush ran to his wagon and brought the bacon and the knife. He stood watching while Butler cut the bacon into small pieces.

"Hold that red ox by the nose and by one horn," Butler ordered rolling up his right sleeve as far as it would go. "Keep his head up while I put some of these small hunks of bacon down his throat, as far down as I can reach. That will help him to swallow them."

"All right, I've got him!" Colin shouted, clinging hard to the struggling steer. "Get away from here, Sebie! All of you get away from here!"

Butler took a chunk of the fat meat, thrust his arm down the animal's throat, and drew out his hand empty. He did this five times. Each time the red ox nearly threw Colin, but managed to complete the process of swallowing.

"That's enough for that one," Butler said. "Now for the other two sick ones."

"Whatever good can the bacon do?" Eusebia asked. "I'd like to know, if you don't mind."

"It forms a soap with the alkali," Butler explained, "and the soap does less harm. In half an hour the three animals may be able to travel again. But, Mr. Brush, if you keep on letting them drink this alkaline water, the bacon will soon do little good. Some of these ponds through here are fairly black with it."

"Lieutenant," Brush replied, "I'm mighty glad you stopped along! Just almighty glad!"

"Come on, Freddie!" cried Lester Lee, as he began to roll up his sleeve. "You'll have to hold our four sick ones; I'm not strong enough yet," and he winked at Ann.

"You must 'ave kept riding right through the very worst of that storm!" Eusebia said to Butler scoldingly.

"Yes," he answered as he looked at Polly. His face now lost its tensely drawn expression, and with a hesitancy he did not often show, he asked, "Would you wear this? I think it might save you from a heatstroke, whereas the bonnet that you always have hanging down your back might not."

He held out to her the wide-brimmed Mexican hat of plaited straw which had hung from his saddle horn. Its sugar-loaf crown was circled by a band of crimson and black.

"See, it isn't even wet," he said. "It sheds water like a duck."

Polly was so surprised that for a moment she made no move to accept the gift, and Ann caught it from Butler's hand.

"Oh, I never saw the like!" the younger girl cried in delight. "Put it on, Polly, quick!" She set it on Polly's head and fastened the straps under her chin. Then she moved back a few steps, clasped her hands, and said admiringly, "I love you in it!"

Butler's face glowed warm and red through his tan. "I brought it up from Mexico," he stated, "and happened to have it along with me now. It's a little large, but the band can be tightened so it will fit you." With that he stepped closer and pulled the band tighter.

Ann was very quiet for a while as she stood looking at them. Then she moved away, but she smiled back over her shoulder.

Polly was embarrassed as she in turn held out a small bundle she had brought from her wagon. "These are for you," she said. "They're boots of buffalo hide for your horse."

"Boots?" Butler repeated. "For my horse?" He was plainly puzzled as he accepted the present, and unfolded and examined the boots.

"He'll need them beyond Fort Laramie," Polly explained. "I happened to notice that he twists his front feet on the ground when he sets them down—after he sets them down, I mean. Long ago my father told me that on the sharp gravel and stones out there beyond Fort Laramie, horses that twist their feet grind their hoofs off till they bleed and become crippled and perhaps have to be killed, unless they are shod or wear coverings like these. Even the Crow Indians put boots of this kind on their ponies."

"I never heard that before," Butler said slowly. "And you made these for me?"

"For your horse." Polly laughed.

Butler smiled at her. "Thank you, Miss Kent!" he said. "Then it's true, of course, that your father was out here with Bonneville."

"Yes," the girl answered proudly.

Brush, who had been watching the sick oxen, stooped to pick up what was left of the bacon, but remained for a time bent over, both hands on the ground. Then with an effort he lifted his hands. With body still bent until his head was only a couple of feet from the ground, he began to move away very slowly, leaving the bacon on the ground.

Polly and Butler were too interested in each other to notice him. But Eusebia hurried to him and held his arm to steady him. Ann, with sudden fear in her eyes, ran to take her father's other arm.

"I like the hat," Polly remarked to Butler.

"And I like the boots," Butler answered.

They looked at each other and smiled again. Then Butler said gravely, "But I came back to tell you that our train is miles ahead now. I'll probably not see you again this side of California."

"Oh, I'm sorry!" Polly answered. "We're going as fast as the oxen can travel."

"I know," Butler said. "But you'll get there sometime. You can't go back. Endless miles of teams are eating down the grass behind us. The best chance now lies ahead of us. And everybody knows that."

"Grass!" Polly exclaimed. "Grass ahead! Nobody thinks of anything else. Once, they could think of nothing but gold. Now it seems as if we have all forgotten that. Only grass is important. How long since you've heard anyone sing, 'Oh, Susannah'?"

"There *is* feed ahead." Butler spoke with hesitance. "Out in California, I'd like to leave a letter for you at Sutter's Fort —if I pass there ahead of you. Will you answer it?"

"Polly! Come!" Eusebia cried. "I need you!"

"Why—why, yes," the girl said breathlessly to Butler.

Eusebia called again impatiently.

"I'm coming!" Polly called back.

"I mustn't keep you," Butler reminded her.

Polly saw that something was wrong with Brush. That was why Eusebia had called, so she went to help, thinking that Butler would wait for her. But when she looked for him a few minutes later, he was far away. She called good-by to him, though she knew he could not hear her.

XV

OUR CRITTERS ARE STARVING

SUDDENLY Mrs. Brush became very busy. She climbed into her wagon, made a mustard plaster, and then took a big blue pill out of her medicine chest.

"You girls run off a ways till I put this plaster on your father," she whispered and called to Colin.

When he came, he made a wry face, but took the pill nevertheless. When he saw the mustard plaster, however, he protested angrily. Sebie paid no attention to this but got him up beside the wagon on the side away from the passing emigrants and stuck the plaster across the small of his back.

"There!" she said. "I wish I could think of something else I could do for you, Colin."

"Something else?"

"I wish I could, Colin."

205

"Thunder and lightning!" Brush exclaimed. "That's enough! Nothing ails me, anyhow! But you keep on, and you'll have me down sick!" He reached a sack from the wagon, dropped it on the ground, and sat leaning back against a wheel, his wife looking at him as if she knew his case was hopeless.

"What's going to become of us?" she moaned when the girls returned. "This going on and on—daylight till dark— day after day! He's all tuckered out! He's not hisself any more!"

Colin looked up at her, shut his eyes, and then shook his head in disgust.

"It's you that's tuckered out," Polly said gently, trying to hide her own anxiety. "The oxen threw him about pretty hard, that's all. He'll soon be over it."

"I'm over it now!" Colin declared as he got up, elbowed his wife aside, and went back to his team. To his surprise he found, after moving about a little, that he could stand straight again. This time he bent over very cautiously, picked up the bacon from the ground, and put it into the wagon. When the sick cattle were able to stand, he swung them off the road and prepared to camp.

Colin was frightened. He had been anxious at times over what might happen to Sebie and Ann if he were to fail them, but he had always been able before to leave his worries behind by thinking about the gold he hoped to find. Now foreboding held him. He could not think of the gold at the end of the journey. He could see nothing ahead but disaster. He tried to decide what to do if his oxen should die. Well, he had money —he could buy another team. But could he? Who would sell?

The other emigrants were all in the same plight as he. Many indeed were far less fortunate. Their teams were giving out, and not one of them would dare to sell him even a single ox or a mule.

He remembered the lone woman he had seen heading home from the cholera camp, and then he thought of Sebie and Ann again. Neither of them had ever even tried to yoke a pair of oxen. What would become of them if he should be stricken —if he should die—before they reached their journey's end? The possibility appalled him.

Polly had driven the animals out on the prairie, searching for grass, and Lester and Freddie were greasing their wagon. Colin watched the boys, depressed by his belief that no one could safely depend on them, and went to the place where Sebie and Ann were getting supper. He intended to tell them both that they must learn to yoke, hitch, and drive the cattle. But before he reached the women, he realized that such a suggestion would frighten them now.

"I'm feeling fine," he greeted them instead. "I only twisted a bone or so making a soap vat in Old Red's insides; but it's all right now." Taking down a milk pail, he started away.

"You stay here, Colin!" Eusebia scolded. "You know you don't need to go. I've got all the good fresh rain water we'll need for everything."

"Exercise, that's all I need, a little walking for a change to limber me up," he answered, and went on toward the river, nearly a mile from the camping place.

"Ann," Mrs. Brush remarked, as she set a pot on the stove, "it's so kind of sociable like tonight with such a lot of people everywhere around us." Then she turned slowly and stood watching the emigrants then passing. In an hour or more they would begin to leave the road for the night. "I wonder," she continued, "how long it would be if we just stayed here and couldn't go on any more. I wonder how long it would be before the very last one of 'em would get past and leave nothing here for miles and miles—only the prairie and the Indians—and us."

"Mother!" Ann cried. "What ails you? Why, I never heard the like! Mother, you mustn't worry like that!"

"Worry!" Eusebia began to bustle about. "Don't you ever think that!" she said scoldingly. "Worry? Why I'm just getting to feel it's nice and friendly to have all those folks everywhere around us, even if they are all strangers and hardly ever look at a body. Why, honey, can't you let me like being amongst 'em, just for the once?"

Before dusk, Murillo and Hedges drew alongside with a single team of eight oxen.

"It's too bad your wagon was struck, Mr. Murillo!" Eusebia said.

"Too bad for *Phoebe Ann*," he answered lightly. "Luckily I had shares in three. A flip of a coin, some complicated swapping, and *Pretty Nelly* came traveling with Gale and me. *La Belle Antoinette* stayed with my recent partners. So everything's all right again, Mrs. Brush, except that now I'll have to buckle down to honest toil."

Colin sat down to talk with Sebie and Ann, who were busy getting supper.

The animals had grazed and were now tied to the wheels or hobbled; and the supper dishes had been cleared away while it was still light. When Brush glanced toward him, Murillo signaled him by a jerk of the head.

"We'd like to travel with you," he said in an undertone when Colin caught up with him. "Are you willing?"

"Well, now, that's—why that's—I'm mighty glad to have you," Colin answered, calling to the women at once. "Here are two more added to the train. Two good husky young travelers, Sebie!"

"Well, that's a blessing!" After Sebie had said this, she looked at the girls, neither of whom spoke. Her expression then changed to one of concern.

Murillo, too, looked at the girls. "Don't vote no, Polly," he said. "Whenever you want any womenfolks to notice you, I'll keep out of sight and hide King Cole in the sagebrush. Besides, all my clothes except these were burned in the wagon."

"It's understood, Mr. Murillo," Polly answered, "that when I go hunting, I go hunting alone."

"I'm darned glad o' that!" Freddie Dascomb put in. "Then we won't have to chaw on no more old buffalo bulls!"

Ann glanced at Hedges, smiled at him, and clung to the older girl's arm.

"Colin," Eusebia said, when no one else was near, "what'd you let them join up for without asking me?"

"You let Lester and Freddie in! Did you say anything to me beforehand?"

"That's different!" she flared. "You know Gale's sweet on Ann. And Bill Murillo's all eyes for Polly. Now you've got the four traveling in the same train!"

"We'll be along, won't we?" Brush answered.

That night the men sat apart from the women.

"It's the worry more than anything else that's the matter with Sebie and the girls," Brush commented. "They've known about too many things that have happened. From now on, we've got to keep 'em from knowing, all we can."

"Guard our talk, you mean?" Hedges asked. "About the alkali water, lack of grass . . ."

"Yes, and everything else that's scary," Brush interrupted.

Murillo arched his brows and shrugged his broad shoulders. "Then I'll leave it to you next time to hide the lightning," he retorted.

Next day, Laramie Peak could be seen eighty or a hundred miles away across the plains. From then on, one mountain after another crept slowly above the horizon as the party advanced. On the seventeenth of June, camp was made on Laramie Fork, a clear and beautiful stream from the southwest. Here, near its meeting with the North Platte, it maintained an average width of twenty yards in its windings among clumps of trees and through meadows abounding in currants and gooseberries.

Fort Laramie was a walled enclosure of adobe which the American Fur Trading Company owned. It stood between the two streams not far from the ford of the Laramie Fork, which was easily crossed. The walls of the fort were four or

15

five feet thick and from twelve to fifteen feet high, backed up inside by terraces. In the center was a clear space of about three acres, and all around this were the quarters for the men.

A few miles beyond the fort, another great stream of teams came fording the North Platte on the old Mormon trail from Council Bluffs and turned into the already overcrowded main road leading on to the West.

In the six hundred miles which the travelers had followed the Platte across the plains, there had been only one creek flowing in from the south for them to ford. Now the country changed. The first day after leaving Fort Laramie, they forded two large creeks of clear, cold water that came from the Laramie Mountains, and crossed three ranges of hills where the ground was the color of red brick. The next day two more streams and several more ranges were crossed. During this time, the road was hard, and on its fine sharp gravel, thousands of animals soon wore off their front hoofs until they stained the ground with blood at every step.

Many of the oxen thus crippled were killed for beef, and some of the mules were shot and left by the roadside, while others were driven on, pieces of blanket wrapped about their injured feet. The boots of buffalo hide which Polly had made saved three oxen in her train. But Colin Brush took time to shoe all his animals. Each ox had to be roped, thrown down, and held by the other men while Colin nailed the shoes on. Two evenings and part of one afternoon were spent at this work.

The road followed the North Platte a hundred twenty-five miles and the day before the party was to reach the crossing of this river, Polly rode on ahead. She found a ferry, a single small boat which could take over, at most, a hundred teams a day, and she saw fully two thousand wagons camped at the river, waiting. Here in the mountains, the stream was too deep and swift to be forded, so the crossing had to be made by boat.

When Polly told Brush, he smiled a little. "Well, we've got our chance now to get ahead of all those teams," he said.

Polly could see that the other men were deeply troubled, but Brush was not disheartened, even when he saw the great encampment.

"Our critters are starving, and it's now life or death," he said without any show of anxiety. "So we'll use my wagon as a ferry. I built it like a boat, that's why it extends out wide above the wheels. All it needs is calking. We'll ferry our freight over, take your wagons apart and boat them across too. Back on the Missouri we couldn't have tried that and come out alive. Here, maybe we can. Anyhow we'll chance it."

XVI

THE BOATWRIGHT'S WAGON

BRUSH turned off the road some distance from the ferry landing, drove almost to the river, and told all hands to tend to the cattle.

"Freddie," he said, when they were through unhitching, "you stay here on guard while Gale and Bill go with me to see what kind of river this is."

Polly was surprised by the change in the man. He spoke now in his accustomed good-natured way, yet decisively.

"I'll run this job here whether you boys find it sets easy on you or not," he declared. "You've all got to jump when I tell you, and keep jumping. This comes close to what I've done all my life. And we've no time to waste.

"Lester, go over there and chop down three little cotton-wood trees which will work up into good strong oars, say ten feet long. Drag back the three pieces, and then you and Freddie start making them." From the river, he called back to Polly, telling her to get on her pony and come along.

The North Platte, a quarter of a mile or more wide, was running full, with a rapid current down the main stream and an eddy almost as rapid swirling up along the bank. Out where the counter currents met were numerous whirlpools.

"There may be an eddy like this on the other side, too," Brush said. "Try swimming across, one of you—whichever swims the best. The other one of you I'll need to help me. Polly, stay right here and watch, to see whoever swims all right. I'll not have time to." He hurried the last few words so much that the girl, who was approaching, could not hear him.

"I'll take the river," Murillo said. "I'm a little better in the water than Gale is. What's the point, Mr. Brush?"

"Polly, you listen, too," was the answer. "I want to know where to push the wagon boat in, how far this eddy will take us before we can get out of it into the main stream, where it's best to hit the eddy on the other side, and where there's a good place over there to land.

'It looks like we'd have to follow a course from here like a letter S—be carried upstream quite a ways, have the main stream shoot us down till we catch the eddy on the other side, and then be carried up to where we can land the boat. See if you can find all that out before dark."

"I'll try," Murillo replied.

"Then Gale and I'll go take my wagon apart, I'll calk the bed, and we'll fill it with water to soak overnight. If it's still full of water at daylight, we'll start crossing then."

Murillo began to take off his boots. "Can you swim, Polly?" he asked.

"If I have to," she answered.

"No, Polly, I don't want you to swim. You mark this place, and stay right here," Colin said. "Watch Bill. See just where the water carries him, just where he breaks out of this eddy, where he gets into the one I think's over there across, and where he lands.

"He may have to swim it three or four times, because, when we get over there, we'll have to know how to bring the boat back empty. When he works the whole thing out, tell me. And, Bill, see how the grass is on the other side. If it's good, we'll try to swim the stock across first thing in the morning and get Polly and Ann over there to stand guard."

Polly, as she watched from the bank, saw Murillo swim steadily across the eddy, and she saw him carried some distance up the river before he struck the main current. When he did reach it, he was sucked under instantly. The girl knew that the water, which came from snow high in the mountains, was cold, and she feared Bill had been taken with a cramp.

Watching the place where he had disappeared, she tried to fix the point in her mind in relation to her own position on the bank and a bluff on the bank opposite, and felt suddenly frightened and helpless. Then the thought came to her that Brush had stationed her here to let him know at once if

Murillo were in danger of drowning, and this frightened her still more. She was turning to ride to the wagon where Colin was at work when she saw a head bobbing about in the main stream far below where Murillo had vanished.

She looked again, saw the swimmer go quartering downstream and once more disappear, this time near the opposite bank. But he bobbed up quickly and was swept back up the river by the eddy to a point nearly opposite her.

Then she saw him wading waist-deep, and she knew that he was looking for a safe landing place for the wagon boat. After he left the water, he spent a long time searching, and then ran up the river nearly a quarter of a mile to a high point in line with herself and the whirlpool that had first sucked him down. At the foot of this bluff he again took to the river, and swam back, keeping in the main current and landing above the eddy that swirled past Polly.

"Best grass you ever saw—no teams—and five antelope feeding over there," he said, when he had caught his breath. Then he went to where King Cole was hobbled, and soon led the white stallion back, saddled. "It's going to be easy, Polly," he declared. "But a lot of hard work, that's all."

Swimming that river had not looked easy to her, but she merely nodded her head and watched, while Murillo swam the horse across the river and back twice. The first time they both disappeared in the whirlpool this side of the main stream, but were not drawn under near the other bank. The second time they were not drawn down at all. After this Bill was ready to report to Brush.

By that time Colin's wagon had been unloaded and its hood removed. The men took down the wagon bed, and Brush calked its seams with cotton batting. This done, he rigged a false bow, which although not water-tight, would lift when running against the current. Colin then bolted an oarlock on each side and one at the stern. Finally he called the men to stop unloading their own wagons long enough to help him slide his boat close to the river. There they filled it with water and left it to soak.

It was then dark, but more than a score of other emigrants had gathered about to watch. Those same men, along with many more, came in the night with their wagons, and next morning Colin and his party found themselves the center of a large camp, which was rapidly growing larger.

At daylight, the water in the wagon box had lowered only two inches. As soon as the men had helped Colin dump the water out, he had Murillo and Polly drive the animals into the river. Bill, on the white stallion, went with them.

Polly's task, after all the cattle had been driven in, was to turn back any that might refuse to cross, but none balked. In five minutes the oxen and the ponies were on the other side in the rich grass, getting the first full meal they had had since leaving St. Joseph. Leaving King Cole there too, Murillo swam back.

Mrs. Brush and Ann had a hearty breakfast ready for the whole party. While they were eating, Colin remarked, "Make a good meal of it, for we'll not have time for another bite till midnight, maybe."

The five men slid the wagon boat into the water, tied it close to the bank with a fifty-foot rope, and loaded in the yokes and chains for the first trip. Brush and Gale rowed. Bill, who knew the currents, steered. The trip was made safely, and the return took only five minutes.

The two girls, together with Polly's rifle and saddle, and as many wheels as the wagon bed would hold, were taken next. Then the running gear, the tools, provisions, clothing, and all the other goods were unloaded from the wagons.

The men worked hard, without resting. Long before noon, the river bank was lined with emigrants busily unloading their wagons and making them into boats, or cutting down cottonwood trees with which to build rafts. Meantime, thousands of oxen and mules were grazing west of the river.

Colin Brush was not the only one who had built a wagon that would serve as a boat. One mule train from Pittsburgh had two boiler-iron wagon beds with sloping bows and sterns. These had been set side by side a few feet apart, and by bolting the two bodies firmly in position with long, flat iron bars, the party would soon have a good-sized catamaran ready for use as a ferry.

When he heard of this, Brush was tempted to go to see the strange craft, but when he learned that it would take him ten minutes to go and come back, he kept on at his own task.

Each time he returned after taking over a load, he was besieged by anxious men begging him to take them across later on. Several times he was offered a hundred dollars a day for ferry service. But Colin was in a hurry.

The sun was still an hour high when everything, except the three wagon beds, had been taken over. These had to be set crosswise on the boat to leave room for the men at the oars. Polly urged that her wagon bed be towed, for she was anxious to find out whether her kegs, three of which were now empty, would keep it afloat. Brush, however, refused to take it in tow.

Even the girl's light wagon box, with its hood off, made the craft top-heavy, but it met with no mishap. Eusebia, who up to that time had been left to guard, went over with this load. When she climbed up on the west bank, she clasped Ann in her arms with as much fervor as if she had not seen the girl for weeks.

The bed of the wagon belonging to Lester and Freddie was carried too far down by the main current, and the men had trouble with it in the eddy, but finally they managed to land it. The *Pretty Nelly* was longer and heavier. Just as it swung in toward the farther bank, it slid, causing the boat to lurch and throw Gale Hedges into the water. The wagon bed slid off with him and began to fill.

Ann, who was watching, screamed, covered her eyes with her hands, and sank to the ground.

The other two women saw Murillo jump to the bow of the boat, untie the rope, and swim with it to the sinking wagon. Fastening the rope to the wagon, he got into shallow water, and by clinging to the line, was able to swing the bed of *Pretty Nelly* against the bank. Meantime the boat, which Colin could not manage alone, had run up through the eddy till it struck the down current. Brush was calling for help.

Polly rode quickly to the bank and followed down the stream. She thought that by swimming beside her pony she might reach the place where she could save Colin. She was about to make the venture when she saw Hedges already swimming far out into the stream, saw him catch the boat as it came down, cling to it, and climb in.

He and Colin each took an oar, and soon the girl could see that they were working their way in very slowly. They landed more than a mile below the new camp. There Polly helped them empty out the water which the boat had dipped when the wagon bed tilted in slipping off.

Then she rode back for the men, all of whom came. By using the rope, they were able to drag the craft into the eddy and to hold it close to the bank the rest of the way up. It was dark when they reached camp, where they found Eusebia and Ann cooking again.

Polly had shot an antelope, and Mrs. Brush announced that she would soon have biscuits and steak ready. Before supper, and afterward until midnight, everyone was busy putting the wagons together and getting in the loads.

"It's three months since we've had to camp alone," Eusebia said. "It makes me kind of scared."

"Camp alone!" Colin exclaimed. "There's eight of us! And all safe across! And hundreds of men on this side guarding cattle!"

"But everybody else is clear on the other side of the river!" she answered. "And it seems so quiet—so kind of lonely here —all by ourselves."

"Do you think you could ever have got across this North Platte alone; just you, I mean?" Ann whispered, as she and Polly were ready to drop to sleep in the older girl's wagon.

"I'm glad I didn't have to try," Polly answered. "I felt so helpless, so no-account, here at this place. But, Ann, we have a good party now, and I think we'll stay together, don't you?"

There was no answer; Ann was asleep.

XVII

INDIANS AFTER ANN

AT FOUR o'clock next morning, Polly had put ponies and the oxen out to feed. Soon after daylight, while she was driving in the stock, she heard a shot off in a small ravine.

After breakfast, Murillo brought Eusebia a haunch of antelope. Turning to Polly, he said, "I find that *I* hunt better alone, too. Mrs. Brush, this may help make amends for the buffalo with which I nearly ruined your reputation."

That day and the next there was very rough wheeling, and no way to get to the road that led west from the regular ferry. No wagons had ever been driven where Brush was forced to travel. This was an anxious time for all the members of the party. They saw no other travelers, and, because of that, feared they were lost in the mountains. Late the second afternoon, however, they came to the road. To their surprise, they found

they had taken a route shorter by many miles than the one
the emigrants from the ferry had followed. The men figured
that by this adventure they had cut their way ahead of four
thousand wagons and were now up toward the lead in the
great migration.

The little creeks they now crossed all flowed south to the
North Platte, from which the travelers were drawing constantly farther away. The route lay through a barren country,
sandy and desolate, in full view of snow-capped mountains
north, west, and south of them. They found good grass beside
the creeks, and although there was not much of it, few other
trains had been along ahead of them with animals to crop
it down. Here antelope were plentiful, and three were killed
in one morning.

On the evening of the third day in this arid region, the
teams were driven into the Sweetwater River not far from
where Independence Rock rises solitary on the plain four or
five miles from a range of granite ridges.

Polly and Ann climbed the rock next morning with Murillo
and Hedges. Then the older girl said she was going afoot
across the plain about five miles to the Devil's Gate, a deep,
narrow chasm, roughly three quarters of a mile long. In past
centuries the Sweetwater had cut this gorge through one of
the granite ridges.

Murillo wanted to go, too, but he'd rather ride, he said.

"There's an Indian trail over the ridge along the edge of
the precipice," Polly told him, "but it's too steep for horses.
If you go, you'll have to walk."

They set out together; and while the teams were going roundabout ten miles or more by the road that led into Sweet-water Valley, the two found the trail and climbed that precipitous path. Frequently they stopped to look down at the river flowing far below between its perpendicular rock walls, sometimes little more than thirty feet apart in places.

At the upper end of the chasm, the walls opened out till they bordered a valley more than a mile wide, a grass-covered valley in which the Sweetwater came flowing straight out of the west. Here Polly and Murillo waited until noon, when the rest of the party overtook them.

The road continued up this valley a hundred miles, first on one side of the river and then on the other. Eight or ten times a day, the members of the party climbed into the wagons and crossed the stream, which was only about a foot deep and at first not more than twenty feet wide. As they traveled up, it became narrower, and on the third day they came into an open country which was bare of vegetation except close to the water's edge.

Here, in a small depression, the emigrants who had passed ahead of them had scraped away six or eight inches of earth in places to uncover solid ice. This ice was as clear as crystal and more than a foot thick.

In two days more, the party arrived at South Pass, the summit of the Continental Divide. There camp was made at Polly's urgence, near two springs, one of which sends its water to the Pacific Ocean, while the other's stream flows to the Gulf of Mexico.

"My father was here four times!" she cried, thrilled at the sight. "I've heard of South Pass all my life! Now I'm here!"

At this high altitude it was very cold, and a strong wind was blowing. The men gathered sagebrush and kept a fire going in the shelter of a rock until bedtime. There was plenty of bunch grass for the animals.

The next day, at the Little Sandy, all decided to take the road to Fort Hall instead of the road by way of Salt Lake which was described in the Mormon Guide Book. After reaching the Big Sandy, they crossed, in two days and a night, the desert-like region beyond, where there was grass but no water. On the fifth of July, they turned their teams into the clear, cold current of Green River, crossing it as they had crossed the North Platte, in Colin's wagon boat. This gave them heavy work again and caused a little more than a day's delay.

Along Smith's Fork of the Bear River, and until they began to climb the mountain that lies between Ham's Fork and the Snake River, they passed many villages of friendly Indians. These Indians lived in valleys so rich in grass that the animals of all trains soon regained their strength and took on weight.

Although the mountains were very steep in places, feed was plentiful day after day. The travelers, believing that all the hardships of the road lay behind them, laughed and sang and shouted as they hastened on. The only glum faces were those of Freddie and Lester, who complained that Murillo and Hedges did nothing any more but scrub up and make love to the girls.

In this mood, the party came to Fort Hall, another adobe-walled trading post. It was owned and still used by the Hudson's Bay Company, and on the surrounding plain, thousands of Snake Indians were camped. Some had horses but many had come long distances afoot.

Polly went to the fort to post letters which would be forwarded, she was told, by way of Oregon. When she overtook the train, she found a score of mounted Indians close around it, riding at the slow pace of the oxen. They seemed friendly and swung their ponies aside to allow room for the girl to ride through the band, which she did with an effort to appear unconcerned. She could see that Colin Brush and the other four men of her party were alarmed and watchful.

"What do they want?" she asked as she passed Gale Hedges.

"Don't know," Hedges answered in a low voice. "The old chief kept talking Indian talk and pointing to Ann, till her mother and she crawled back under the canvas to keep out of sight."

"Come up here, Polly!" Brush called. When she rode forward to where he was walking beside his oxen, he said, "Tell the boys we'll keep traveling till we see a big party of emigrants going into camp; then we'll swing right in among them."

"Go up to the chief and scold him," Polly urged. "Tell him to go away. Indians like people who aren't afraid of them. If he doesn't mean trouble, he may go if you tell him. If he does mean trouble, we'd better have it now in the daytime while there are hundreds of wagons within sight."

"I don't know what is best to do," Brush answered.
16

For ten or fifteen minutes the girl rode on in silence. Then she turned her pony, rode back, and stopped in front of the chief. He reined in his horse, and sat facing her, the other Indians drawing up around them.

"We don't want you so near our wagons!" she scolded. "Stop following us!"

The chief, old and deeply wrinkled, sat very straight on the strong black and white pony which he was riding bareback, Indian fashion. He was small and dark, wore no paint, and only one long feather. His hair, plaited in two queues, was drawn forward over his ears and hung in front of his body. The Indians around him were all dark and small, but their hair hung loose about their faces, reaching to their shoulders.

They all wore long, close-fitting shirts of tanned skins with porcupine quills fastened along the seams at the sides, long leather leggings fringed with what looked like human hair, and moccasins decorated with figures made of porcupine quills. Polecat tails hung from the heels of some of the moccasins.

The chief wore a tippet, and Polly thought it the most beautiful Indian garment she had ever seen. It had a collar of otter skin, the tail forming one end and the nose and eyes the other. From this collar hung all of two hundred small quills of white weasel skin closely rolled around twisted cords of silk-grass. These rolls of ermine, or white weasel skin, fell from the collar almost to the waist, forming a handsome short cloak.

The chief looked at Polly for a time, then for a full minute spoke to her earnestly in his own language. She caught no sign of menace in either his voice or his gestures.

"I can't understand," she answered, and pointed toward the mountains. "Don't follow us! Go somewhere else!" With that she turned and rode slowly after the wagons.

The Indians moved out of the way of the oncoming trains, remained in a group beside the road for a time, and then rode off.

In the evening, when the Brush party was in camp, the chief reappeared with five members of his band and an old mountain man riding a saddled horse and leading a scraggy pack-pony.

"My name's Jed Ensley," the mountain man announced as he was dismounting. "Don't git yer dander up about ole Chief Scar Lip. He's a good Injun as Injuns go. A Shoshone. Yere's how 'e figgers. The white nation's crowdin' the Injuns plum off'n the yarth. Only thing to save 'em is fer the Injuns to git 'em some smart white chiefs to l'arn 'em to live like the white nation.

"Way to git smart white chiefs is to git a white wife. Way to git the wife is to trade ponies fer her, er steal her. The whiter the skin, an' the yallerer the ha'r, he figgers, the whiter an' smarter the chiefs that'll be their children. You got one o' the kinds 'e wants—not fer him—fer any lucky, good-lookin' young chief she happens to want fer her'n. They'll treat 'er good."

"We don't care to trade," Brush answered, hiding his anger because of his anxiety over the danger to Ann.

"That's jest one thing an Injun don't never onderstand. A squaw's a squaw—to be traded fer—er to be run off with if'n 'e can't make a honest trade." Ensley looked steadily at Brush. "An' that last's the part I come along a-purpose to warn ye."

Other Indians had ridden up, a few at a time, until almost the entire original band was gathered about. In addition several white men from trains camped near had come over and were listening, for the presence of Indians always interested the emigrants. Many others were coming, also, most of them with their rifles.

"What can we do to keep them from bothering us?" Polly asked.

"*Ye* ain't in no danger." Ensley grinned at her. "They got black-headed squaws'n to spare. The yallerer the gal's ha'r, the more near white 'er sons'd be, an' to their thinkin', the more sartin to save the tribe. We can't stop 'em wantin' to trade."

"I can!" The voice came from the crowd of listening emigrants, and the man who spoke turned and went briskly toward a near camp.

"Go slow thar!" Ensley warned. "An' one to a time!" Looking at Brush, he said, "You talk—keep talkin'—so it'll look right when I tell 'em, long an' perlite, why ye ain't out fer a trade. He'll give ye two hundred ponies fer 'er."

Brush wet his lips and began to explain, but his talk was disconnected and halting. When he had finished, and Ensley was speaking to the chief in the Indian language, Polly felt her arm caught in a firm grip. She turned to find herself facing the man who had left the group a few minutes before. He was tall and dark, with piercing black eyes.

"Go bring the yellow-haired girl out of the wagon," he whispered. "Have her stand in front of the chief, about twenty feet from him. Warn her and your men not to be scared at what I do. I'm a prestidigitator by profession—a sleight-of-hand man. In two minutes these Indians won't want the girl."

Polly, impressed by his air of confidence, brought Ann over, pushing her forward until she was facing the chief.

"He wants me fer to tell ye he'll give three hundred ponies," Ensley said.

The tall man with the piercing eyes stepped up beside Ann, opened her mouth and looked into it for a few moments, apparently with extreme caution. Then he dangled a piece of red rag in front of her lips.

Suddenly he seemed to seize and drag out of her throat what looked like a live, brilliantly colored snake, which wriggled and writhed as he held it by the neck and the tail.

Ann shrieked and drew back horrified. Polly, with an arm about her, steadied and quieted her. The sleight-of-hand man shouted something, and a thin youth, as solemn as an owl, quickly set a box with a hinged lid on the ground. When he raised the lid, the man thrust the snake, still wriggling, into the box.

The lad clamped the lid down and carefully carried the box away, while the man stood wiping his hands on a soiled bandanna, gazing at Ann with a look of extreme distaste. "Ask the chief if he'll give three hundred and fifty ponies for her, now that I've taken one of her snakes away," he announced in a loud voice.

Ensley turned to the chief and spoke rapidly, but the chief's face remained expressionless. In a moment he mounted his pony and rode off, followed quickly by the other Indians.

"Professor, that's the best show I've seen you put on yet!" the sleight-of-hand man's friends guffawed when he stepped back among them.

"Mighty bad medicine you make, feller!" Ensley added. "That passel o' Injuns won't never come back."

A grave, gray-bearded ox driver, who spoke with mellow, full-voiced ease, declared whimsically, "Gentlemen, we have just seen a kind of thing that has made history all down the ages. That Indian is a patriot, trying zealously to save his people, and he was defeated by a trickster's cunning." He smiled at Ann. "Nevertheless, this flaxen-haired miss is to be congratulated."

"I know how you feel, Mister," another emigrant called to Brush. "I got word of this chief back along the line, and when he come, I kep' my little towhead down inside a barrel in the wagon. If I was you," he added to Ann, "I'd do my hair up and pull my sunbonnet down close till I got out of these parts."

Ensley then spoke to the group: "You're headin' into trouble. The half o' you won't never git your wagons down the Humboldt an' across the desert. You got three weeks travel thar in the ash heaps o' hell. Pack animals kin make it, but me, I wouldn't risk haulin' no wagons. Git packs an' travois poles ready afore you leave the mountains. You'll need 'em. Leave your wagons—leave 'em behind, men—afore the heavy loads kill all your beasts off. An' fill your water bar'ls where the water's good. The Humboldt River's pizen."

"Fella name o' Butler had a right smart notion back at St. Joe," someone remarked. "Wanted scouts out sendin' word back of what we had ahead. We should o' took 'im up."

Ensley mounted and rode on toward Fort Hall, many of the men walking for some distance beside him, asking anxiously about conditions along the river he had named. During five days of travel beyond this place, which was near the American Falls of the Snake River, the members of the party went unmolested; but their way lay through a rough and difficult country. They climbed high mountains where ice formed at night, and they made perilous descents into hot valleys.

From one mountain top they could see a number of wagons wrecked beside the road below. To prevent the same fate befalling theirs, Hedges and Murillo felled several pine trees eight inches across the base and twenty-five feet long, then carefully cut off all the branches six inches from the trunk, and chained a tree so it would drag top-foremost behind each wagon. After that they rough-locked the wheels, and each driver, with only a single pair of animals hitched to the wagon, slid his load down into the deep valley through a cloud of dust that sometimes almost completely hid everything before his eyes.

During the fifth day, after their meeting with the Shoshone chief, they saw, many miles to the south of them, part of the long caravan of gold seekers that had taken the Salt Lake route, creeping over a ridge on its way to the Humboldt. In

the evening they themselves camped beside that river well up
near its source, where the stream was so narrow that they
could jump across.

Here, more than eight hundred miles from the place where
Murillo and Hedges had joined the party, the men cut travois
poles and filled Polly's empty kegs with clear, cold water before
venturing into the great, arid valley of the Humboldt, which
would lead them on into a desert. And here, as she tried to
sleep, Polly was depressed for the first time in her life by a
sense of being alone. She felt that she was going out all by
herself into a land unknown and perilous. Until now, she had
been pushing on with confidence day after day in places made
fascinating and familiar to her by her father's tales of adventure.

But now she was going where he had never been. From the
high mountains he had veered to the north and west: and
the party that Captain Bonneville had sent exploring down the
Humboldt had left a vague, poorly reported record of appalling
hardships, dissensions, inhumanity, and disaster.

With all the hundreds now plodding along the trail ahead,
and the thousands coming on from behind, the girl could not
rid herself of her haunting sense of loneliness. Her sleep that
night was troubled.

XVIII
THE RIVER OF DEATH

THE four wagons jolted down the mountains along the course of the river, descending rapidly the entire first day. Where camp was made, the river ran thirty feet wide, and the water was pure and cold. Emigrants had been streaming past for several days, and the grass, which had been good, was now eaten off until nothing was left for the oxen or ponies. The animals of the other trains that camped near by fared no better.

The second day was intensely hot, and the cattle, weakened by lack of food, moved slowly, their tongues hanging out, and had to stop often to rest. Polly thought her ponies suffered less because they held their heads higher than the oxen and so breathed in less of the alkaline dust. They had hardly covered ten miles when night halted them where there was no

235

grass at all—nothing for the oxen and horses to eat except some willows which grew along the water.

The third day was hotter still; and the whole aspect of the country changed. Instead of mountains, a dreary plain lay ahead as far as the travelers could see. Away from the stream this plain was bare of all vegetation except sagebrush.

When the teams had gone about five miles, Brush let them rest, and the worn-out creatures all lay down. As there happened to be willows here, growing on the river bank, the men decided to stay where they were until night. Then they would hitch up and see if their spent oxen would travel better when the sun was down.

Many other weary emigrants and exhausted teams camped that day beside the river. Those who still kept to the road formed only a straggling line with open spaces between the slowly moving wagons.

Brush and the others of his party started when the sun was still an hour high, and as they had the moon for nearly three hours after dark, they easily kept in the road and held to a good gait. At midnight they turned the animals out for an hour, braced themselves with strong, hot coffee, and traveled until sunrise, when they found a little grass and plenty of willows. After a good breakfast, they lay under their wagons and slept a couple of hours, until the intense heat wakened them. From then on, they were so bitten by ants and annoyed by maddening flies that they could neither sleep nor rest. By noon they could see the heat rising from the plain in waves, as it sometimes rises visibly above a hot stove. The outlook

over the country was the same as it had been the day before—
desolate in the extreme.

Near where they were camped, they found the first of the
many victims of the plain which they were to see: an ox that
had mired and died at the edge of the stream. A short distance
up the river from where the ox lay, they obtained their water
supply. At sundown, they went on, resting an hour at midnight and driving until the sun was an hour high. Conditions
where they stopped this time were worse than they had been
at the last camping place, and the outlook was worse. Here
they found six dead oxen and two dead mules, the first dead
mules they had seen on the Humboldt plain.

"Our only consolation," Brush said to Hedges, "is that
while these other folks make only ten or twelve miles a day,
we cover nearer twenty at night. But can we stand three weeks
of this? It will take us that long, for our teams are slowing up."

Gale did not answer his question.

Murillo and Gale drove the animals to the river to let them
drink. It was a loathsome stream, rapid and full of dangerous
whirlpools. The water felt slippery and had a peculiar sickening taste, but nearly all the travelers had nothing else in which
to wash, or for drinking or cooking. The members of Polly's
party were fortunate, however, for there was still a supply of
pure water in her whisky kegs.

Along the bank of the stream, the willows had been cut, and
there was no grass. On the other side, Hedges spied a good
patch of grass. But as he and Murillo were about to turn the
cattle back toward the wagons, they saw two new graves, each

with a name, a very recent date, and the word "drowned" scrawled in pencil on the crude headboards.

Nothing was said in camp before the women or Colin about either the graves or the grass. All the men, except Brush, slipped away with sickles, swam across the river, and floated back as much grass as they could handle. They knew that Brush was not a strong swimmer, and they agreed among themselves that all the grass that came to the camp from the other side of the Humboldt they would bring.

They all tried to sleep, but again the heat, the ants, and the flies caused them to give up in despair. Somehow they worried through the day, and could hardly keep their eyes open when they started on that night. Until nearly two in the morning they had the moon with them, and they were able to make good time, though all the cattle that had drunk the alkaline water several weeks before now began to show signs of giving out, and had to be tied behind the wagons.

The travelers knew that these animals were being sickened not only by the water but by the dust, which had by this time become a thing of horror. On this plain, which never seemed to have been moistened by a drop of rain, the road had been cut by wheels and hoofs into fine alkaline dust from four to ten inches deep. As the weary oxen dragged their feet through it, it rose like a vapor, enveloping them and everything near them. The eyes of all the emigrants grew inflamed, their noses became sore, and their lips cracked open.

Fear and despair now traveled in all the slow-moving trains; and with many went sickness and destitution. In a number of cases, food, shoes, and clothing now sorely needed had long ago been discarded to lighten the loads.

So far, the road along the Humboldt had followed close to the stream, which had never been more than six or eight feet below the level of the plain, but one morning, when Brush and those with him looked for the river, they could not find it. They traveled until the sun was more than an hour high, and at last found the stream in a gulch ninety feet deep. Leaving the wagons on the high ground, the men and Polly drove the animals unyoked to the water. With the exception of a few willows on the bank, there was no vegetation anywhere in sight.

In the water Polly counted nine dead oxen and five dead mules in all stages of putrefaction. That day she opened the second of her water kegs, but the river, which often thereafter flowed deep in a gully far from the road, continued to furnish the only supply of their livestock.

Travel now became more difficult, for the country ahead was wrinkled with sun-scorched, barren hills that taxed the strength of the weakened teams.

Another day of scarcely any sleep followed, and Eusebia was so overcome that Colin would not let her cook the meals. The men also were too weary to putter about a fire, and after this they, as well as Mrs. Brush and Ann, lived chiefly on Polly's parched corn while it lasted. Most of the bacon, of which only a small supply remained, was to be saved for the oxen, and there was no game.

It was impossible for anyone to sleep except at night; consequently, as soon as the teams were hitched that evening, Brush

and the three women tramped ahead three or four miles and
threw themselves down by the roadside. In a moment they
were asleep, and they slept soundly, until wakened by Hedges
when the teams came up to them. Then they started on
again.

Night after night, from midnight until morning, they drove,
Murillo, Hedges, and the boys taking short naps in the same
way. Often those walking beside the teams fell asleep as they
tramped along and were wakened only by stumbling into a
sagebrush or against an ox. Each succeeding day seemed worse
than the last. To the heat, the alkaline dust, the ants, and the
flies, was soon added an all-pervading stench from dead oxen
and mules, the number along the way becoming terrifying.
Everywhere, as more and more animals in the teams gave out
and were left at the roadside where they fell, hollow-eyed,
exhausted men could be seen through the vaporous dust,
breaking up their wagons to make packsaddles for the oxen
or the mules that were still able to carry burdens.

Brush seldom talked now, and Lester Lee, always so good
natured, grew morose. Neither of the two boys ever seemed
fully awake, and it became almost impossible to rouse Lester
from his roadside naps. Polly tried in vain to rouse him one
night as the teams passed where he lay asleep. At last she
lifted him to his feet, but he reeled, fell against the end of the
last wagon, and struck her a clumsy blow in a sudden rage.
Thinking that his own exertion had wakened him if her efforts
had not, the girl turned away from him and plodded ahead in
the dark.

Whether Lester lay down again or at once wandered off, he himself never knew, but sometime in the night he found himself approaching the river in a broad path. In the darkness he could see ahead two persons standing, one on each side of the path. As he was about to walk between them, one of them raised a club to strike him. At that instant he saw that they were Indians, so he turned and fled, the two following him, whooping and yelling. How far he ran, he could not tell, but just as his strength was gone, he reached the main road and fell unconscious in a camp.

Even Freddie Dascomb did not miss Lester the next morning, but took it for granted that he was busy at some chore. At noon, a passing train stopped, and two men helped Lester, still weak and nervous from fright, out of a wagon.

"Why didn't you wake me?" he demanded, glaring at Polly. "It was your turn!"

"I got you on your feet and thought you were wide awake," she answered. "What happened? Where have you been?"

"You did not!" he cried in anger.

"He run into our camp toward daybreak and dropped in a faint," said one of the two men. "It took 'im most an hour to come to, and then he said Injuns had chased 'im."

"Last night Indians ran off all but eight of the sixty oxen belonging to the company next to us there," Murillo volunteered. "They're Digger Indians. This is their country we're in."

The members of the company to which he pointed had chopped into their wagons for wood with which to make pack-saddles, and their eight remaining animals were loaded now with food. The men planned to drive the oxen until they dropped, and then go on with such packs as they themselves could carry. Soon after they had gone, Polly went over to the wagons they had left.

"Brush don't want his womenfolks to know, but half of our steers are about done," Hedges said to her when she returned.

"I've been watching," she answered. "Gale, I've moved two one-hundred-pound boxes of hard bread and eight sacks of flour to the back ends of those first two wagons so that you can fetch them away quickly. If you can get them over here before anyone else takes them, we can soften the bread for the animals, and later on make the flour into a kind of gruel for them. That's what they need—they must have something nourishing to eat."

"That's a find!" Gale exclaimed. "I'll bring them."

"Not alone!" Polly cried, as he started away. "Get the other four men together! All of them! Hurry! And all of you work as fast as you can. These other people are too worn out to think of rummaging; but as soon as they see what we've found, they'll come. Their cattle are starving, too."

By the time the food had been removed and stored away, a dozen men were hunting in the abandoned wagons.

Just before making camp that morning, the party had crossed a brook. Polly, on her pony, scouted up it now and found that a mile away, where it formed a pool surrounded by willows, the water was clear and good. Returning to camp, she told the men about it.

"We've been too lavish with water," she said. "Five of the six water kegs are already empty. This is probably our last chance to fill them with water we can use. Several trains are camped close to that spot, so we'd better not let more than one keg be seen at a time. Some of these people look mighty desperate."

Brush and the two boys drove up the brook with her wagon and the kegs, while Murillo and Hedges herded the cattle to the pool to let them drink there instead of at the river. Before he left, Murillo had insisted that Polly rest. Soon after he had gone, however, a man approached her.

"Somebody says you've got kegs—extra kegs," he began. He stood looking at her with burning eyes. "I'll give you fifty dollars for one."

"We haven't any extra," Polly answered, "only what we need ourselves."

"A hundred dollars for a keg!" the man continued. "A hundred and fifty dollars for one that smells fresh. Our barrel stinks from the foul water it's held. It stinks so bad it makes all of us sick."

"We couldn't spare one keg for all the money you might name," she answered, as she turned to avoid the appeal in the stranger's eyes. After a long last look at her, he walked away slowly.

"That's the most terrible thing I've ever had to do," she said aloud to herself when he was out of hearing. "But we do need all the kegs! We do need them!"

When it was time for the men to return and they did not come, she grew anxious and went over to the place where the

17

kegs were being filled. There she found Murillo and Hedges on their knees facing each other, Colin Brush lying between them.

"What's happened?" she cried.

"We found him this way," Hedges answered. "He's not dead; but we can't revive him."

Polly saw then that the side of Colin's head was covered with blood and that the men were pouring water over his face. There were no kegs at the pool, but in her wagon Polly found five that were full and carefully covered. In a moment she saw Lester and Freddie coming and hastened to meet them. She could see that Lester was still in an ugly mood.

"We mighty near landed another hundred pounds of hard bread," Freddie called. "While Brush was bringing down the last keg, a fellow told us what wagon the bread was in and all. When we got there, though, somebody must have beat us, for there wasn't . . ."

"Wait a minute!" Polly interrupted. "Where are the other four kegs?"

"There in the willows," Freddie told her.

"I can't find them," she answered. "What a terrible thing you have done—to go away, leaving Mr. Brush all alone like that! If the kegs are in the willows, come and show me."

They returned to the pool, but there were no kegs.

"What did you do?" Hedges demanded when he found that Brush was still unconscious. "Why did you run away?"

"You mean we did that to him?" Lester cried furiously, almost weeping in his sudden rage. Without warning, he struck

Hedges in the face. Gale in turn knocked him down. He let
Lester get to his feet and then knocked him down again.
Freddie started to help his friend, but Murillo held him.
Lester clinched on getting up a second time, and in a moment
he and Hedges toppled into the pool, which fortunately, was
not very deep.

Gale struck the boy again, reached for an overhanging
branch, and pulled himself out of the water. But Lester
floundered about in the pool as if he were stunned, until
Murillo went in and brought him to land.

"Four kegs are gone," Hedges said. "I've looked all
around."

At Murillo's suggestion that Mrs. Brush might have some
stimulants, they lifted Colin into the wagon and started with
him to camp.

XIX

THOSE PRECIOUS WHISKY KEGS

THE men bandaged Colin's head and laid him under the shade of a blanket hung between the upper edge of his wagon bed and stakes driven into the ground. Then Eusebia filled a spoon with something which she forced between her husband's lips, sat down in the dust beside him, and began to wave his hat above his face to keep off the flies.

"Ann," she said in a little while, "you sit and watch your father."

The girl took Eusebia's place and began waving the hat. "Mother," she called presently, "don't fuss so over that hot stove. When he comes to, and sees you working like that, he'll be worried."

"If he does come to, he'll need something strengthening—he's bled so much," Eusebia answered calmly.

Murillo and Hedges went to hunt for the stolen kegs. When they returned after a fruitless search among neighboring camps, they found Colin's condition unchanged. Their clothes were still wet, their frayed flannel shirts, caked with greasy dust, were steaming. Their trousers were in tatters halfway to the knees, as were those of nearly all the other men who had reached this stage of the journey. For days no one had wasted strength digging into a loaded wagon for a change of clothing. Neither Murillo nor Hedges even thought now of changing.

"You'd better stay around here in case of need," Bill suggested to Gale.

The cattle and the ponies had been driven back from the pool and were now tied around the wagons. Some of the steers were lying down, others were stamping and moving restlessly, tormented by the ants and the flies. The heavy odor from their sweaty bodies and the smell of fresh dung made the stench from the dead mules and oxen along the roadside and the river seem less sickening now.

Gale Hedges sat down across from Ann, took Colin's hat from her, and began to fan him. The girl started to weep silently, and suddenly she threw her arms about Colin and lay with her face against his breast. He had not moved nor opened his eyes since he had been injured.

"O Father, I wish we had told you before!" Ann sobbed. "I couldn't bear for you never to know! Gale loves me! We're going to be married!"

"Well, now that's fine, Daughter!" Brush answered in a strangely feeble voice.

Ann sat up startled, and found him looking at her. "Father!" she gasped.

He drew a deep breath and tried to rise, but lay back, wincing in pain. As he looked at the girl, he seemed to have trouble getting her within his range of vision. Finally he said, "Daughter, that takes a heavy load off my mind."

"Don't try to get up," Hedges urged gently.

Brush turned to see where this voice came from. "Well, Gale, I didn't know you were here," he said, lifting a hand to his head. He felt the bandages there, and after a moment of surprise, ran his hand slowly over them before he added, "If anything happens to me, you'll look after Sebie, too, won't you, Gale?" Despite all efforts to keep him still, he sat up.

"O Mother!" Ann called. "Father's awake!"

Eusebia, her back toward them, cast a frightened glance over her shoulder and almost stealthily lifted a pot off the stove before she turned. She wiped her hands carefully on her dusty apron as she went to where the others were.

"Sebie," Brush said to his wife, his voice stronger, "see if you can't rig up a regular meal. I'd like to eat something just once, like we used to have at home."

"You—you—want me to?" and she burst out crying.

Brush started to get up, and Hedges and Ann helped him to his feet. At first he was weak in the knees, but he soon grew steady.

"I'll get the meal," Ann offered.

"You can't cook like your mother can," Colin chuckled. "But if you don't feel up to it, Sebie . . ."

"I want to!" sobbed Mrs. Brush. She started back to the stove, but stopped. "You feeling all right, Colin?"

"Mighty near starved is all." In a lowered tone to Ann, Brush almost whispered, "This you told me—is it a secret?"

"Mother knows," the girl smiled.

"Run along then and help her." After Ann had gone, Colin asked, "Gale, why have I got this bandage on?"

"Someone must have hit you a deuce of a rap on the head. Don't you remember about it? Out there by the pool."

"I was toting a keg down to where Lester and Freddie were —and when I got there—why, that's all I remember till I woke up just now."

"Didn't you see anybody? Somebody you thought was Lester or Freddie?"

"They weren't there. Nobody was. They'd gone. There was one keg—only one keg." Then he began to look troubled.

"Well, don't bother any more about it," Hedges urged. "You're back in shape. Somebody hit you, and we brought you here. Ann was telling you we are in love with each other. I meant to ask the first chance I got if you'd be willing for me to marry her."

Colin Brush, at all times of a serious mein, had smiled hardly at all during the past week. Now he had a broad grin on his face. "Gale," he answered, "I bet I've told Sebie a dozen times that if I was out hunting for a son, I'd dog your trail. And she never told me! I'd have made oath she couldn't keep a secret like that. Yes, sir, that's a good one on me!"

"Thank you!" Hedges said as the two shook hands.

"So somebody hit me." Brush kept on smiling. "That's funny! I didn't have a dollar on me, and my watch was hanging in my own wagon. I guess I've started being lucky for a change."

In a few minutes he began to walk about, went to his cattle and looked them over carefully. The younger man, made curious by this unusual good humor, followed him. But Brush seemed to have recovered entirely. After a whispered talk with Ann, Hedges went to hunt for wood for the open fire over which he was boiling water to soften some of the hard bread.

In the dusty road off a distance from the camp, an ox was down. Colin went out there. Drivers from the rear of the train, impatient over the delay, were coming to see what was wrong, and there was much loud talk. The fallen ox was one in a train of five wagons, no one of which had more than four animals left, and most of these were in poor condition.

After a hurried conference, the men of the train hauled their wagons to one side to unhitch, dragged the ox out of the road, and got out their packsaddles, which they had in readiness.

"Knew we'd come to it," one of the men called to Brush.

"You've got four cows," he answered. "They're too small to carry heavy loads."

"Got any big, strong oxen to trade?" the man asked sarcastically.

"I can spare you four," Brush told him. "We're fixed so we could do just as well with cows. Leave their yokes on and come over and look at the steers."

"What do you think of this?" the man asked two members of the train who had been listening. In a suggestive way, he pointed to his own head, calling attention to Colin's bandages.

"Let's have a look at the steers," one of them answered.

The three went with Brush, looked over his cattle, and made an even trade. Then they drove his four heaviest oxen away, adjusted the packs on them, and loaded them hastily.

Colin was very careful to lead the four cows so that his wagon hid them from the women. He tied them where the oxen had been, and then went around to where he could watch Eusebia and Ann prepare the meal. He laughed and talked gaily, but did not mention the trade he had made. From time to time he would walk slowly around the wagons to look at the cows, and just as slowly return. Ordinarily he never found a moment for idling; now the thought of finding something to do did not occur to him.

Polly, returning hot and staggering tired from a vain hunt for the kegs, spoke to Lester and Freddie without receiving an answer. Later, while she was talking to Brush, telling him she was glad he had not been badly hurt, Hedges came with an armload of wood for the stove, and Murillo rolled up one of the wheels that had been soaking in the river.

"Father doesn't know the kegs are missing," Ann whispered. "He seems so kind of happy that we thought we'd not tell him till later."

Polly took some of the softened bread, which had cooled, to her ponies, and let them feed. After Murillo had given some bread to their cattle, Gale noticed that Brush had not fed his animals, and went off with two of the kettles.

"Say, Mr. Brush!" he shouted in a moment. "Look here, will you?"

"I know. I traded." Brush walked toward him.

"Traded!" Hedges cried. "You traded your big oxen for four cows?" He stood looking at Colin with narrowed eyes.

"I told you my luck had changed!"

"Where are the men you traded with?" Hedges steadied his voice to keep the anger out of it.

"Went on half an hour ago." Colin smiled gleefully at the younger man. "Gale," he said, "you think a minute. You've seen a lot of dead oxen, even mules, hundreds and hundreds of them. Seen any dead cows? No, sir! And the dead oxen are the big ones. Noticed that? They're the ones that give out. The small cattle, the small mules, are the ones that are standing this trip—the cows, best of all."

Hedges, who was studying Brush anxiously now, had failed to notice two men standing beside him.

"He's right!" one of the men exclaimed. "Smith and I both figured that out six or eight hundred miles back. How are you anyway, Gale Hedges!"

Gale turned and stared at him. "Well, Billy Bell!" he cried.

Bell laughed. "I'd never have known you from your looks," he said. "But I heard you holler out just now, and it struck me I'd heard that voice of yours before." He and his companion were carpenters from Rock Island.

"How far back did you leave your wagons?" Murillo asked, after the greetings and the introduction were over.

"Wagons!" Bell exclaimed. "How these people are suffering because they brought wagons! Why, you couldn't count the thousands we've seen abandoned after the teams had killed themselves hauling those terrible loads! No, sir, we left Council Bluffs the first of June with a saddle horse and a pack horse apiece, and I'm betting we'll be at the mines a week before you are."

"We left camp opposite St. Joe the tenth of May," Murillo said. "And I for one haven't thought of the mines for days. We'd have turned back a dozen times if we had dared."

"But you folks way up here in the lead are lucky, too," Bell told the listening group. "You're far enough ahead so you've missed the cholera. Back yonder, all the way from this side the Missouri River on out to Fort Laramie, the road is lined with the graves of them that took the cholera."

"Have you seen any other Rock Islanders?" Hedges asked.

"Not a one," Bell answered. "But how many of the people you pass do you notice now? And how many would you recognize in their dirt and whiskers and scarecrow clothes? I heard your voice; and then I heard somebody call your name."

The two carpenters hastened away, and after they had gone, Hedges gave a feed of bread to Brush's cows, as well as to the two oxen still left in the team. As he fed them, he noticed with interest that the cows were not so sluggish as the steers in fighting off the flies.

Just before sundown, Brush himself yoked up. As he and the women started ahead for their brief snatches of sleep at the roadside, Polly saw that the boys had not yet begun to get ready to go with the party.

"Hurry, Lester!" she called.

"We're stayin' right here till morning!" Freddie answered. "Now on, we travel days. An' what's more, we're for the road that goes by the Truckee River. You can go by the Carson if you want, but we talked to a man who knows."

Polly walked back to them. "Don't be mad about what happened," she said. "I'm beginning to think we're none of us responsible any more for what we do. Come on and get your oxen hitched."

Murillo, who had followed her, took hold of her arm and led her away. "No use," he said. "Gale and I've tried. We've tried every way we know how to keep them from cutting loose. They'll not listen."

"But that will make it hard now for the rest of us," Polly said."

"Yes, till Brush gets right again. That bump on his head has left him a skitterwit. You women can't risk it off alone with him on the road at night. He'd be no protection. And we can't leave him as the only man in charge of the teams."

"But we'll have to keep on traveling at night! Bill, we'll have to!"

"Gale and I will drive till midnight, while the rest of you try to sleep in the wagons," he answered. "At midnight we'll shift; but you can call us if anything goes wrong. If the extra loads kill off the teams—well, we can't help that. We must all sleep; and in the daytime, in this hole of a place, we can't."

"All right," Polly agreed, stopping beside her ponies.

Moving at a snail's pace, the party arrived at the Sink of the Humboldt at dawn, after eighteen days and nights of travel down the dreadful valley of the loathsome river. Each succeeding day had seemed worse than the last. They still had all their animals and their wagons, but they had little more than one keg of water left.

They found themselves beside a marsh in which the Humboldt sinks into the desert. This marsh, with no outlet, appeared to be fully fifteen miles wide and of much greater length. The briny water was from three to six inches deep, and in it grew coarse grass nearly four feet high.

There must have been a thousand wagons already camped on the higher ground about the Sink. Thousands of oxen and mules were out in it feeding. Hundreds of men were cutting the grass, dragging it out, or carrying it to where it could be spread in the sun to dry.

At the edge of the desert, Hedges and Murillo, following the example of others, dug a well in which they found the water was less alkaline than that in the marsh. The animals were given all of it they could drink, were fed heavily with fat bacon, and then turned loose to munch the coarse grass.

The desert, no doubt once the vast, level bed of a lake which had dried up, seemed unendurably hot, even in the early morning. A short distance from where the party halted were several wells of boiling water from which steam was

rising constantly. Polly saw some of the younger members
of a near-by train boiling coffee in one of the wells, by letting
their pots stand in the edge of it. Following suit, she filled
Mrs. Brush's pot with water from a keg, put coffee in it from
her own small store, and set the pot in a well to boil.

Men who were at work in the marsh said that about half
the weary emigrants intended to take the route to the Truckee
River. Brush, Hedges, and Murillo decided, however, to let
their teams feed and rest until the evening of the following
day, and then to strike across the desert toward the Carson
River seventy-five miles away.

XX

LIEUTENANT BUTLER PASSES

THAT afternoon, Polly was busy beside her wagon on the dry ground near the edge of the Sink. She took out the poles the men had cut for her in the mountains, and rigged two travois for herself. When she was sure they had been securely fastened and were ready for loading, she roped two kegs in each, and in one she put a hammer and a shallow stew-pan. In one of the kegs there was a little more than a gallon of good water. When Gale Hedges called to her from where he was turning over the grass he and Murillo had cut in the marsh and dragged out to dry, she was spreading a blanket over this load.

"Not going to travel squaw fashion, are you?" Hedges asked.

Polly held a finger to her lips and pointed warningly to Brush, who was tossing restlessly beneath the wagon in which

257

Eusebia was trying to sleep. Hedges stopped turning the grass and came over to where she was working.

"Gale," she said in a low voice, "you and Bill, and Mr. Brush too, are making a mistake when you think this desert will be easy to cross. My father, though he was never here, was certain that the stories the Indians told about it were true. It won't be easy. If we make it—all of us—in the condition we're in, we'll be lucky."

"The road's hard, Polly,"—Hedges answered. "Bill's been out quite a ways to see, out a mile, he thought, and from there on ahead it looked good and hard. He says it's mighty hot, but that we won't have much trouble, that a single yoke of cows could haul either wagon."

"It's not the road," the girl continued, "nor the weight of the load. It's the terrible heat there—the lack of water—and our animals. Weak, nearly starved, so sick from the alkali in the dust and the water that bacon grease can't save them any longer."

Hedges shook his head at her frowningly. "I know some of the cattle can't make it," he answered, "but at least we can try to go on with what we've brought this far. Other people are trying it."

"What do they know?" asked Polly as she looked about over the sweltering camp. It was a camp in which there was little stir of life. The men at work seemed to be merely dragging themselves about; the others lay in their wagons or underneath them. There was no shouting, no laughter or singing, and no braying.

"What do they know?" the girl repeated. "No one has come back to us out of the desert to tell us about it. You've heard these emigrants talk. They thought the Humboldt plain was the desert. How many knew when they got here that they'd still have the real desert to cross? Let's not fool ourselves. I'm going tonight."

"Why, Polly!" Hedges exclaimed. "Our stock must have another full day's rest. They must have! They couldn't go anywhere as they are."

"My ponies can, I think. Some of the cattle may be able to make it, too, after another day here with rest and feed. Maybe they can, even hitched to wagons. And maybe not. If not, what about Mrs. Brush and Ann? They've been a long time on a short ration of water. Can Mrs. Brush walk seventy-five miles now in that desert without water? Without *water?*"

"You mean you're leaving us?" he asked, his speech slow and spiritless.

"I'm starting tonight," the girl announced. She spoke with effort and without emphasis, as if the matter had only a faint, impersonal interest. "I'm taking four kegs, two in each travois, with a little hay and eight loaves of bread, for myself and the ponies. If I get through to the Carson River where there's good grass and no alkali, I'll let the ponies drink and graze to strengthen them. Then I'll come back to meet you in the desert with water you can drink." She paused as if she expected him to say something, but he stood looking at her.

"It's thirst people die of in the desert," she continued. "I'll try to meet you in time. But, Gale, don't attempt to

18

cross tomorrow. Wait till the evening after. Give me two full days of rest before I start back from the Carson."

"Good Lord!" Hedges muttered weakly. "You must think it's going to be terrible!"

"I must have some hay roped over the kegs to hide them, besides what the three ponies will need. I don't want anybody crazed with the heat out there to think I have water."

"I'll cover them; but, Polly, you're not the one to go," Hedges objected. "And it's not so bad as all that. Nothing like. What you're planning is for me or for Bill, not for you."

"Sakes alive, Gale!" Polly replied with a trace of irritation. "What are you thinking of? *You* have the other two women to look after, and Colin Brush besides. Look how weak he is." Her lips were cracked and swollen, and her eyes ached after working in the sun—the inflamed lids thick and heavy.

Hedges, looking past her, saw a bony white horse with drooped head plodding along away from the marsh, dragging a travois filled with wet grass. A man in tattered clothes was leading the horse.

"I'm going to tell Murillo about this," Gale said.

"I don't want to talk to him about it, to him or anyone," Polly answered. "I want to rest from now till nearly time to slip away. It's getting late. I must go as far as I possibly can tonight." She climbed into her wagon. The heat under the canvas cover was stifling, but she straightened her bedding and lay down. When the man with the bony, white horse reached the higher ground where the grass was drying, Hedges was beside him.

"Bill," he said, "Polly's set to cross the desert alone tonight, so she can meet us with water from the Carson."

Murillo straightened and stared at him. His beard had grown, and he was thin and haggard. "We've water enough, if we use it sparingly and travel at night," he answered. "There must be nearly three quarters of a keg left. We've crossed one desert, and we'll know what we're about when we cross this one."

"She's made up her mind, and is nearly ready," Hedges told him.

"She's not going alone!" Murillo cried.

Hedges lifted his hat for a moment and ran his hand back through his hair.

"But, Bill," he said, "it won't be one of us *and* Polly crossing the desert, if that's what you mean. It'll be one of us alone or else Polly alone. I'll flip a coin with you . . ."

"Your place is with the Brushes, right along with them, Gale."

Murillo looked a long time at King Cole. He laid a hand on the sweaty side of the stallion. The hot skin under his fingers sank deeply between the ribs and did not move freely over them. "I'll talk to her," he said at last.

"I wouldn't!" Hedges urged. "There's only one way to stop her—drive off with her ponies while she's asleep."

"I'm not doing anything, not anything at all, that Polly wouldn't like; and she wouldn't like that. I won't trick her." Murillo started to drag the wet grass from the travois, but stopped and turned back. "I must talk to her, Gale," he said. "I can't put it off any longer."

"It may be too late . . ." Hedges hesitated, looked at his friend, and for a moment seemed not to know just what to say. "Bill," he got out finally, "somehow I think it will be too late for you to stop her from going—after you talk to her."

"I'm going with her! It's a job that . . ."

"Bill," Hedges interrupted, "before you rush into this, I wish you'd talk to Ann."

"It's a job for two anyhow, bringing water back for the others," Murillo went on. "You four won't have any trouble getting the wagons to a place where we can meet you. The whole thing's needless, but if she's set her mind on going, why—anybody's desert is no place for a girl to cross alone. I'm going to talk to her, Gale, and have it all settled right now."

Hedges took the grass from the travois and scattered it in the sun. Then he loaded some that was dry to use in covering the kegs, and led the stallion to the wagons. The work there took him longer than he had expected it would, and after he had finished, he went to the marsh. As he was wading out from where he had been cutting grass, he came up beside a man who was driving a worn-out packhorse and two pack mules: a man he recognized as Lieutenant Butler. The Lieutenant had grown a beard and was covered with sweat-soaked dust from his trip over the Humboldt plain.

Butler noticed Hedges, glanced back, and then spoke. "Have you seen anything of the Brushes?" he asked after a few words of greeting. "Our party went by way of Salt Lake. We were delayed, and the boys decided at last that it was everyone for himself. Then I heard of a girl and three ponies on ahead—and tried to catch up—to help, perhaps, crossing the desert."

"Murillo and I've been traveling with Polly and the Brushes since the day the lightning struck Bill's wagon," Hedges told him. "They're yonder, up on the rise."

The two men went on together. When they came near Murillo, Butler talked to him a very short time, and then turned to Hedges:

"I see Miss Kent's wagon now. I'll go on and see her."

"Don't!" Murillo put in quickly. "Don't disturb her. She's asleep. She and I are striking into the desert tonight without the others, and she needs rest."

Hedges saw Butler's whole body grow tense, his bloodshot eyes open wide. His swollen lips closed tight for a moment. Then he asked quietly, "You're joining up with her?"

"Yes," Murillo answered. "Unload your beasts and camp with us. They look tired."

"I'm not halting," Butler replied, as he nodded slightly to both men and left.

"I'm glad it's settled!" Hedges spoke with unusual warmth. "My congratulations!" He held out his hand.

Murillo shook his head. "It's settled," he said, "but I've not spoken to her yet."

Hedges looked at him in surprise that turned to deep concern. "Then I'm sorry you told Butler what you did," he said. "I thought—and he must think—it was settled for always, not just for the trip to the Carson." He turned and looked after the Lieutenant, then back to Murillo. "Bill, you'd better have your talk as soon as you can."

Before Butler reached the Brush camp, he saw Polly get out of her wagon. A moment or two later he drew up a few steps from her.

"Good evening, Miss Kent!" he said.

"Why, Lieutenant Butler!" the girl exclaimed.

His poise, his well-kept air, despite the Humboldt dust and weeks of travel, reminded Polly at the moment of his service as an army officer. He was still wiry and fit looking, and had not changed so much as the other men had. In contrast to his appearance, the thought of her own disregard of looks after the recent hardships of the road was disturbing to her.

"You've kept well to the front." Butler spoke with cool precision and came no closer to her. "Most of the crowd is behind you—strung out for hundreds of miles, I believe," he said without smiling.

Polly was struck by his aloofness. "Are you camping?" she asked.

"Merely stopping for a moment as I pass. You're going on tonight?"

Polly glanced toward the Brush wagon. "Yes; but they are not," she said in a lowered voice. "The Brushes don't know about it yet. Won't you stop and have bean soup with us?"

"Thank you, no. It's better not."

With the flat of his hand, he slapped the pack horse, which moved away, followed by the mules. He took off his hat to the girl, then turned and fell in beside his animals.

Polly, with both hands clenched, stared after him. Ann, who had been unable to sleep, came over to where she was standing.

·"What is it?" the younger girl asked. And in a moment, "What's the matter? What *is* the matter?"

"Nothing!" Polly answered dully.

"Who was it?"

"Lieutenant Butler."

Both girls noticed that he had taken the road leading into the desert toward the Carson. Ann, after watching him, turned again to Polly. ' What happened?" she asked.

"Happened?" Polly, meeting the other girl's anxious eyes, suddenly gathered her thoughts. "Nothing," she answered, with what she meant to be an air of unconcern. "He just stopped a moment in passing."

She stooped over the nearest travois and felt for the kegs under the hay that Hedges had roped over them. Then she went over to the kettles in which hard bread had been left to soften and then to cool, and carried three of them, one at a time, to her horses. While they were feeding, she remained near them to see that nothing was wasted. All the dried grass she had placed before them in the early afternoon had been eaten, except a few wisps. These she picked up and placed in little heaps beside the kettles.

Bill Murillo and Hedges came over to where the two girls were standing. Hedges took Ann by the arm and led her away.

"Polly," Murillo said, "you're not going out alone tonight. If you go at all, I'm going with you—but . . ."

"No, Bill," she interrupted.

"Polly, I know you've always thought me a frivolous fellow, out for any good-looking girl that might happen along."

"I was mistaken," she replied.

"No, I was what you thought me—till I fell in love with you. When that happened . . ."

"Oh, don't!" Polly interrupted again, almost wildly. "I know how fine you are! One of the finest! But I'm not in love with you; and I've tried to make you see all the time that I'm not."

They stood looking at each other, both very unhappy and both very near exhaustion.

"It wasn't your fault," Murillo said at last. "I didn't want to see. Wouldn't let myself. I always take too much for granted. I'm the overhopeful kind, Polly."

She could not bear to see him trying to smile to hide the hurt. "I'm sorry!" she murmured. "I wish you could know how terribly sorry I am." Then she turned and left him standing beside her ponies.

"Are you going with her?" Hedges asked, when, a few minutes later, he found Murillo in the same spot. But he needed no spoken answer. "Listen! Listen, man!" he went on. "This is not the time to tell you such a thing, but it's not the time to keep silent either. I've just talked again with Ann. It's Butler that Polly's in love with. Ann told me. She's thought so a long time. Now she's certain of it."

"Butler?" Murillo looked at his friend with surprise, as if he thought he had mistaken what he had heard. "But he hardly more than stopped to speak to her, barely more than spoke, and went on . . ." he exclaimed.

"You'd just told him that you and Polly were leaving the rest of us—starting off tonight—just the two of you. You told him you were joining up with her."

"Butler!" Murillo repeated the name after a long silence. "Then I've made a mess of things for *her!*"

As he stared across the scorching desert, he could see several figures away beyond the few wagons that were making an early start on the same road.

"Here's the coin," Hedges said. "Heads I go . . ."

"You're out of this, Gale!" Murillo drew a hand wearily across his forehead. "And Butler—does he care for her?"

"Ann's sure he cares. And her mother, too, is sure," Hedges told him. "Polly looked like death when he'd gone; but she hasn't a word to say about what's happened."

Murillo walked away slowly, then called back, "Thank you, Gale!" A short time afterward, mounted on King Cole, he leaned down as he rode past Hedges and said, "If he cares for her as I care, he'll come back for her."

XXI

POLLY GOES ON ALONE

WHILE Hedges was out in the Sink after the cattle and before any of the others of her party were stirring, Polly drove quietly away from the camp. She did not know that Murillo had followed Butler toward the Carson.

It was an hour or more before sundown, and she could see many wagons far ahead, as well as many others starting away from the marsh in front of her and behind her. These wagons were easily hauled, for on this road which was as hard and as smooth as a floor, the wheels did not sink at all. From the cattle that were being urged out into the flat, shimmering desert, however, came a low bellowing, unlike anything the girl had ever heard.

There was no dust, the dragging ends of her travois poles leaving only faint scratches on the fine, firmly packed sand.

Polly kept the ponies going, slowly but steadily.

The ponies moved slowly, but she kept them going steadily far into the night, until they showed signs of exhaustion.

When she let them rest, they stood with heads hung low. She remained standing beside them, knowing that if she were to sit down, even for a moment, she would fall to sleep. The hours when the sun was gone were precious, she realized full well. She did not halt again until past the middle of the next forenoon, when one of the ponies stumbled and refused to get to its feet. All around her here, Polly saw others unable to travel in the deadening heat. Many animals were down, and some that were still alive had been left behind by their owners, who had plodded on with the food they were able to carry on their backs. Within half a mile, there must have been more than a hundred fifty wagons, many of them deserted. And in this distance three or four hundred dead oxen, horses, and mules lay, giving up their stench.

The heat of the sun was worse than anything Polly had ever imagined. It seemed like a heavy burden weighing down her head. She managed somehow to loosen the shafts of the fallen pony, and to drag them off without getting them broken; then she fed some hay sparingly to both horses.

At this place, several wells had been dug by men desperate with thirst. She dragged herself to one of the wells and found the water like brine. A man lying at the edge of the pool told her that the water in all the others was the same.

The girl went back to her ponies, lifted the poles of one travois onto the load of the other, and spread her blanket over them. Under the blanket she lay sheltered from the burning sun; but the heat and the torturing flies made sleep impossible.

That day, from the patch of shade under her travois poles near the salt wells, Polly saw a number of men die. Whether they were the victims of sunstroke or exhaustion she could not tell. Comrades covered some of them with the alkaline earth; others lay like the fallen mules and oxen.

Just before sundown, the girl crawled from under the blanket, loosened the bung of the water keg with the hammer, and poured out some water into the shallow stew-pan. In it she moistened a bit of bread for herself and a loaf for each of her ponies. As soon as they had fed, she started on again.

At midnight, when next she halted, white moonlight flooded the desert. During this brief time of rest, a pack train passed going toward the Humboldt Sink, the mules and the men walking briskly. Polly heard the exclamation: "A woman!"

One of the men came back and told her they were Mormons returning to Salt Lake from the California mines. "You'll make it! And you're far in the lead!" he told her. "Not more than five hundred wagons have gone this road. There's grass and water ahead—grass and water and *gold!*"

He took out a heavy pouch, poured flake gold from it into his hand, and held it out before her in the moonlight. He saw her glance at it without interest, so he returned the gold to his pouch. "We keep showing that to the men we meet, to revive their hope and spur them on," he stated. "Don't give up! You'll make it!"

"Have you water to spare?" she begged.

"Not a drop!" the Mormon answered. "We've nothing to carry it in. But there's plenty ahead. We left the Carson well fed and strong—men and mules—able to push all the way across the desert without a halt. That's the only thing—go fast—spend little time here or the heat will get you!"

"How much farther to the river?" Polly asked him.

"Only twenty miles, girl! You'll make it!" he assured her. Then he hesitated. "The last ten miles, you'll travel through loose, heavy sand, beach sand, like the shore of a lake," he told her. "When you come to that—stop! Rest there! Stop and rest your horses! Don't forget! It's heavy, heavy going!" With a wave of his hand, he set out after his companions.

As Polly urged her ponies on, she could see the roadsides littered with stalled wagons and dead animals. Some teams were still moving, but so slowly now that she passed many before daybreak, though it seemed to her she was only creeping. The oxen did not bellow now. With their heads down and their tongues hanging, they kept up a continual moaning.

When the merciless sun was an hour high, Polly came to the place of which the Mormon had spoken, the shore of a lake which had become a desert. At every step the ponies sank four or five inches into the heavy sand. Finally they stopped, refusing to go any farther. Then she gave them the last of the bread moistened by the last of the water, and with difficulty swallowed a little of it herself.

Both ponies lay down after they had eaten. She tried to get one of them up, but fell herself, exhausted by the effort. How long she rested there in the scorching sand she did not know.

Two men close by unhitched their two oxen. They seemed to be a strangely long time doing it. They did not speak to Polly, nor did they appear to be aware she was there, but she kept herself awake watching them.

She watched them cut several large loaves of bread into very small pieces and feed the pieces slowly to the animals. Next they tied a bag of the hard bread and a slab of bacon to the yoke, which they had left on the necks of the cattle. Then one of the men wrote something on a slip of paper and stuck it on the front of the wagon with a pin.

Trying to think why he had done this, the girl stopped watching for a time. It came to her at last. They meant to return for the wagon, and were giving notice that they did not want anything taken from it while they were gone. When Polly looked again, the men and the oxen were wading slowly on ahead in the deep sand; and she was frightened at being left alone, though she knew she was not alone.

She was on her feet again, but the pony that had fallen beside the salt wells the day before refused to make any effort to get up. At last she put a piece of sagebrush under his tail and touched a match to it. He came to life then, and was soon standing beside Keiëta.

Even these hardy little horses of the plains were now walking skeletons, and the girl had to let them rest every few hundred yards. By noon she could not speak to them above a whisper. Her tongue had swelled until it filled her mouth.

Soon she began to pass wagons which, although deserted, had not been moved to one side but were still in the road—a pair of oxen dead in their yokes in front of one, a mule in its tugs in front of another. But she found that the wagons were not all deserted. A man lying underneath one opened his eyes and made a sign for water. Farther on, a woman sitting alone under the shelter of a canvas cover wearily raised a hand to her lips, from which came a sound that was hardly human.

Beyond the wagons, Polly passed, from time to time, men who had lain down beside the road to die. She stumbled by, or sometimes she stopped to look, haunted by the delusion that here might be someone she knew. The desert and everything in it had begun to seem unreal.

Once her travois pole dragged against a lone man apparently dying. His long body resembled Bill Murillo's. The hat, the ragged clothes, the blackened canteen that lay near, were his. Polly stopped to look. His eyes, his nostrils, and his mouth were filled with bluebottle flies that swarmed out as he gave a final gasp.

Fear took possession of the girl, but she was sure this was a delusion. She knew that Bill Murillo was at the other side of the desert with the Brushes. At length she forced herself to turn away, but the horror of that delusion stalked her. It left her presently, and to her came in the scorching heat and glare of the desert and out of a blurring memory, vague, elusive glimpses of her father whose path she had followed through so many of the hardships and dangers of this terrible adventure.

He had always been to her the one of dauntless will who had never faltered. It was in such form he seemed to come before her now, a heartening presence more real than any of these others; a presence that sustained, in her desperate need, something within herself which she had so long admired in him.

A few hours before sunset, she saw trees which appeared to fringe a river. They, too, could not be real she thought. When her staggering ponies suddenly lifted their heads and started forward so fast that she could not keep up with them, the thought came to her that they had smelled water.

All at once her feet lifted out of the weighted sand and touched hard earth. She knew then that she had crossed the desert, and she marshaled her will to reach the river.

Her thickening, hardening tongue pushed out between her lips, and she could not draw it in. At every step she struggled for breath. She walked—she crawled—her one thought—water!

XXII

BACK INTO THE DESERT

POLLY could not remember how she had reached the river. She found herself lying in it, her head resting well above water. Her tongue and her throat were still so swollen that she could not drink. Near by her two ponies stood belly-deep in the stream, their heads plunged under the surface. From time to time one, and then the other, would raise its head to breathe, and with a snort, plunge it into the water again.

As Polly lay there, one of her vagaries of the desert came back to her—a delusion, she thought it—of a phantom Lieutenant Butler helping her, lifting her when she fell and gently laying her here.

She knew that she must drink sparingly when she could drink at all; but she followed the example of the horses and buried her head repeatedly in the soothing stream.

Until nearly dark, she lay there and, on awakening, found that her ponies had not moved from where she had first seen them. Now, however, their heads were raised and their tongues were no longer hanging. She got up weakly and called to Keiēta. The mare came to her, and Polly laid her cheek against the side of the faithful beast's head and caressed her. Then she drove both animals out beyond the trees and the brush that lined the river, and watched them rush into grass as high as their knees. After this she rested again. That night, for the first time in several weeks, her sleep was unbroken.

She slept until early next morning, but was too tired to eat or to move from where she lay, so she slept again. When she wakened next day toward noon and looked around, she found herself in a grove of cottonwoods beside a beautiful river little more than thirty feet wide, in which unbelievably clear, cold water flowed lazily with hardly a murmur.

Except where the road came down to the ford, the brush along the bank was of such a dense growth that a horse or an ox could not break through it except in a few places. In the water scores of wheels lay soaking, and out in the grass many mules and oxen were grazing. Along the stream in each direction from her were wagons—eleven she could count—and in the trampled grass around two of the ones nearest her she could see men sleeping.

Every part of the girl's body was still stiff and sore, but her mind had cleared, her eyes now pained her less, and she could walk without much effort. Suddenly she saw her travois and went to them. She had not thought of them before; in fact she could not even remember unhitching the horses from them. While she was unroping the kegs to fill them with water, she found the bacon that Hedges had placed under the hay for her. After resting several hours more, she cooked several strips of the bacon held on the end of a stick over an open fire, and ate without discomfort.

The food strengthened her; and she was able to fill her four kegs, roll them from the river, and fasten them again under some of the coarse grass from the Humboldt marsh which had not been eaten. Then she set out to find her ponies.

When she looked up the valley, which was not more than a fourth of a mile wide, she saw a few wagons and many emigrants asleep or resting in the shade, together with several hundred animals grazing. A man she spoke to told her there were two hundred men and a few women then at the Carson.

The ponies had not wandered far. As she was driving them back to the place where she had slept, a man rose from beside a pack lying under a tree only a short distance away. She had not noticed him before.

"You've revived more quickly than I," she heard him say. His speech was blurred, and he spoke slowly.

She looked at him, but made no reply.

"But you came alone out of the desert," he added.

"Yes, Mr. Butler," she answered, bowing her head. "I was lucky."

He seemed to be waiting for a further statement from her, for he did not move from beside his pack. "I . . ." he began, "I very nearly died of thirst—pushed on too fast—till one of the mules gave out. Then I was more careful. But I must not keep you standing." He moved back a step.

She lifted her head and was about to follow her ponies when she heard a throaty voice behind her say, "A moment wi' you, Mr. Butler!"

There was a vaguely familiar Scotch trill in the speech, but Polly gave no further heed. She let her ponies drink their fill and led them away from the river. Then she heard Lieutenant Butler coming. He called to her. Before she glanced toward him, she stooped to lift the shafts of a travois.

"Surely you're not going on with so little rest!" he protested.

"I'm going back into the desert with water. Mrs. Brush, Ann, some of the others—Gale Hedges and Bill Murillo—will need it."

Astonishment grew in Butler's eyes as he gazed at her. Suddenly he grasped the shaft she was holding and pushed her hand away from it. "I'm going with you," he said.

She shook her head in refusal.

"I'm going with you," he repeated.

"Mr. Butler," she asked scornfully, "what's happened to you in the last few minutes?"

"I received a message."

They stood looking into each other's eyes, how long neither knew; but Butler broke the silence. "Well," he said gently, "I'm not hiding it, am I? Till now, I've thought I must hide it." Holding her in his arm, he lifted her chin, compelling her to see what was in his eyes. "Polly," he declared huskily, "I love you! Does it matter to you at all? Does it?"

Slowly Polly's eyes filled with tears, and she hid her face against his shoulder. Holding her so close that it hurt, the Lieutenant raised her head and kissed her.

"Oh, don't! Don't!" she cried.

Startled he drew back a little and looked at her.

"Oh, don't look at me, either!" she sobbed. "I'm such a fright! My eyes—my nose . . ."

Hushing her and taking her in his arms, he whispered, "Nothing could change you to me, Polly—ever! Nothing matters but that we're together!"

"Yes," she murmured. "Nothing else matters. I'm only being silly and vain."

Butler still held her close. "I'll always see you as I saw you when you stopped me that day in St. Joe," he said. "Always, Polly!

"About the message I received . . ." Butler caught himself up. He was silent a moment, then he said hurriedly, in a low tone, "No, not now! Someone may die of thirst while we stay here."

"Oh, tell me!" the girl urged. "The message brought you to me! What was it?"

Slowly he took his arms from her. "There are some things about it I don't understand," he answered. "I don't want to think of it now. Let's get ready to go."

Polly managed to curb her curiosity. "I've two kegs of water in each travois," she said.

"My animals have drunk, grazed, and rested," he told her as he hitched her ponies. "I'll get them and overtake you."

She was halfway to the sand when he came up behind her. The mule and the horses knew the desert now, and refused to go into it. They planted their forefeet, drew back, and refused to budge. But at last the ponies started and Butler's horse fell in behind them. The one mule he still had, followed. When they had settled down to a steady gait, Butler drew off the road and caught up with the girl.

"Did you see anyone you knew out here?" he asked.

"Oh!" she cried. "I couldn't have! But I had terrible fancies! I thought I saw Bill Murillo! But, of course, I couldn't have. He's coming on now with the others. You're making me see something I've tried to forget! I thought I saw him die! But it must have been someone else. I was touched by the sun."

Butler walked beside her in silence, looking straight before him. "Do you remember where that happened?" he asked at last.

"There were so many! But that one—not far ahead, I should think."

"The sun in the desert does strange things to a person," he remarked, after another few minutes. "You come on slowly through this shifting sand. Don't take it too fast; I'm going ahead. I've a canteen filled with water for any poor fellows we meet. When the water is gone, I'll wait for you and refill the canteen from the kegs."

He speeded up and soon left her. Two or three times, she saw him give water to several men who were trudging along. Once she saw him, far ahead, lift what appeared to her to be the body of a man and carry it away from the road. She saw him heaping sand over it with his hands. When he had made a considerable sized mound, he waited for her to overtake him.

Soon afterwards they met a train of four wagons. The four teams and the four men trudging alongside seemed to be making good time. The men nodded as they passed.

"We picked up a woman and three men," one of them said to Butler.

"Where are they?" Polly cried. "Let me see them!"

Two of the men halted their wagons and Polly climbed up the wagons and looked in. When she got down, she shook her head at the drivers and then went on.

"Where did they get water?" she asked Butler presently.

"They reached the Carson three days ago," he told her, "rested, and went out early this morning to bring in what they had left behind."

Beyond the loose sand where the road was hard, Polly and Butler began to meet men with loaded pack animals and some with wagons. They spoke to everyone, made inquiries, and gave warning of the ten-mile stretch of sand ahead.

Along the trail two hours after dark, Gale Hedges answered Polly's voice. She did not know his voice, it was so hoarse and muffled, but he had recognized hers. He had come through with all the wagons, Polly's in tow behind his own and her third pony following.

"Better stop here for awhile," Butler suggested, and when Hedges assented, he led Brush's team off the road. All that was left of the team were the six cows. Hedges had only four oxen, all of them barely able to stand.

Ann came up to Polly out of the darkness and clung to her without speaking.

"The others have to ride," Hedges explained.

Polly took the canteen, made Ann sit beside her, and moistened the girl's lips and tongue. Later Ann was able to take a few drops into her mouth. Polly then did the same for Hedges, who had waited. Butler came back to them after helping Colin and Eusebia wet their mouths and try to drink a little.

"Of course you've seen Murillo," Hedges said, when he could speak without too great an effort.

Polly looked up. The canteen dropped from her hand and lay, the precious water spilling out on the desert.

"I covered his body with sand a few hours ago," Butler answered sadly. For a moment no one spoke. Presently Butler went on, "MacTaggart, the man with the donkey, saw him early the morning of the day before yesterday, and left him beside the road. Murillo had insisted that he would soon be able to go on, but he had given MacTaggart a message for me. Back at the salt marsh, where I passed you going into the desert, he had told me that Polly was going on with him. He knew I had misunderstood, and wanted me to know that, at the time, she had intended to go alone, that afterward she had refused to let him go with her.

"The message was that he had made a mess of things, that he had tried to overtake me and explain. And he sent word that I must turn back to meet Polly. He said that at last, when he found he could not catch me, he hadn't dared to turn back himself, because he feared he might become a burden to her. I received the message only this morning."

Polly stood up. "But you did come out to meet me!" she said tensely.

"I was watching for you, for you and him, but you came alone. Several men who had lain down in the sun to die revived after night fell, and straggled in . . . but he was not one of them."

"Then nothing I saw was a delusion!" Polly covered her eyes with her hands, and while the party rested, no one spoke again.

XXIII

TOO WEARY TO FIND GOLD

TOWARD the end of a two-hour wait, Hedges got out the poles he had stored for a time of need, and hitched Butler's horse and mule each to a travois.

A mother and two children, members of a party whose last team had fallen, rode all the rest of the way. So did Eusebia and Ann, but the others dropped down on one travois or the other whenever they felt their strength giving out.

There was water now to spare. Polly and Butler drew it from the kegs for famished travelers. Sparingly, here and there, they gave it to a mule, an ox, or a horse that looked as if it might be able to drag itself, and some emigrant's last little store of food, out of the desert.

At the edge of the sand they left the wagons, after Polly had pinned notes on them saying the owners were coming

285

back to get them. The party, together with all the animals, arrived at the Carson soon after sunrise. Next day at noon, Butler with the filled kegs, and Hedges driving the oxen and the cows, struck back into the desert. That night they brought in the wagons, from which nothing had been taken. Along the way they picked up nine men.

At the Carson, Polly and all the Brush party, now reunited, rested until the afternoon of the second day following. While they were getting ready to resume their journey and while the men were rounding up the strayed cattle, a little girl approached with slow steps to within a few yards of where Polly was busy with some mending. As soon as Polly spoke to her, she came close and sat down.

"Are you going soon?" she asked.

"Very soon," Polly told her.

"If he doesn't come, I'm to go with you," the child said, her tired eyes filled with misgiving.

Polly knew that three men who had staggered after her out of the desert without animals, wagons, or food, had drowned themselves when they realized their situation. Only an hour before, the body of one had been dragged from the river for burial.

"Has he been gone long?" Polly asked the child.

"A very long time," the little girl answered sadly.

"And he said you were to go with *me*?"

"He said you would take me if he didn't come."

"What's your name, dear?" Polly asked gently.

"Corinne."

"I mean—all of it."

"All of my name? Till we came to the desert, it was Corinne Stuart," the child answered. "Now it's Corinne MacTaggart."

Polly stopped mending and sat as still as the child. "If he doesn't come," she said at last, "you may go with me." Though she set to work with her needle, she kept watch for the little man with the big red beard. He came leading a pony when Hedges brought the last of the cattle.

"You stay here, Corinne," Polly told the child, and went to meet him.

"So soon?" he said. "I hae been gone under an hour—and she came to you. But that is ower long if the bairn is alone."

"Tell me about her," Polly begged.

"A voice called in the desert! I keeked about, dovering. A waur day I hae never known! Ay, 'the name is MacTaggart,' I gie back into the stour. And there one told me he was William Murillo, that on a time had a white stallion. Wad I take a message to Husted Butler? And wad I bring out the child, for now he that speaks is ower weak to carry her?"

"You know that Bill Murillo is dead?" Polly asked.

"Ay."

"You want me to take her?"

"I hae come back," he answered. "Had I not, only then wad I hae you take her."

"But if you wish me to . . ."

MacTaggart lifted a hand. After a moment of silence, he said, "William Murillo took the bairn at the mother's pleading.

All she had else were dead. He waited till the mother, too, departed, then he brought Corinne—tried to bring her. Miss Kent, I hae had no bairn of my own these seven years, till, in the desert, she put her hand in mine."

"We'll be ready to start in about an hour," Hedges said to the Scotchman as he passed where the two were standing. "But Butler says we'll wait till you round up the rest of your ponies."

"Husted Butler wad hae me journey wi' him now," Mac-Taggart explained to Polly. "That is for Coreen—Corinne!" he corrected quickly. "Coreen is not her name! No—Corinne! She howks at my pronunciation.

"Hark!" he cried out, as a donkey brayed not far off. "Wee Jock! He gets his voice again! Since he came to the Humboldt, he has been silent. Now I will find the ponies. They stick to Wee Jock like burs." Dropping the halter rope of the one he was leading, he hurried off along the river, searching in the thick brush as he went. An hour later, he was back with each of his four remaining ponies hitched to a well-filled travois. The little girl was soon nestling among the bundles of a much lighter load behind the gray donkey.

There was now no haste. The four men and the three women walked and did not speed their teams. For them these were days when the gold ahead held no allure and they rested frequently. They slowly climbed the abrupt eastern slopes of the Sierras, relayed their wagons up steep mountains, camped early, and slept late. Rarely did they speak of Bill Murillo, but he still traveled with them in their thoughts.

Polly had been keenly aware of her surroundings and of all the incidents and pressing needs of each day and hour, but now she gave them little heed. Quietly, without comment, and almost without her noticing it, Butler took over her tasks and made travel as easy as possible for her. She was growing strong again, but some of her hardiness had been left behind in the desert.

She and those who accompanied her were fortunate. They had food enough to last them; and they shared it at times with emigrants who had none. In their slow, halting journey of three hundred miles, they came upon many who had left the Carson destitute, and half-rationed themselves so there would be more food to share with the starving folk they overtook.

Without eagerness, dully, wearily thankful to have left behind them the dust and stench of the trail and the deadening heat of the desert, they drew near to the once alluring land of gold. Near the crest of the range they spent an entire day traveling between lofty cliffs, crossing and recrossing a swift little stream in a narrow canyon six miles long and strewn its entire length with boulders.

Another day of steep climbing brought them to where a slide had exposed a smooth wall of rock twelve feet high and more than fifty feet long. On the face of the rock, at no great distance away from the road, had been painted the names of trains that had passed, the number of wagons, and the dates of their passing. The earliest entry, which was made with black paint, read:

TRAIN FROM
JACKSON COUNTY MISSOURI
60 PACK ANIMALS
AUGUST 5, 1849

All the other entries were in white lead, a keg of which had been left beside the wall with a brush. According to this registry, some sixty trains had passed. Among the last entries was this:

OFFSHOOT FROM ROCK ISLAND TRAIN
TWO WAGONS   —
AUGUST 25, 1849

There was nothing to indicate who the members of the "offshoot" were. Gale Hedges took the brush and printed:

MIXED TRAIN
3 WAGONS
2 PACK ANIMALS
5 TRAVOIS
8 PEOPLE
DETROIT
SOUTH BEND
TERRE HAUTE
EUROPE
CINCINNATI
ROCK ISLAND
AUGUST 28, 1849

Next morning, six days after these travelers had left the edge of the burning desert, they found ice three quarters of an inch thick in their water buckets beside this wall of records.

After crossing a great field of ice and snow, with towering mountains north and south of it, they came to the western edge of the Sierra Nevada's crest, from which they could see far out over the numberless peaks and ranges that dropped away lower and lower to the distant foothills.

They rough-locked the wheels and cut pine trees to drag topforemost behind the wagons. Thus checking their speed, they followed the windings of the road down a series of steep descents without mishap. Where they crossed the Carson Valley, they came upon men from thirty or forty wagons who had out their rifles, threatening vengeance against a band of several hundred Indians who had driven all their cattle over a high cliff during the night. From the brink of the cliff, the travelers could see the Indians feasting on the oxen a thousand feet below.

At a fork in the road down in the foothills, a man waist-deep in water in a ravine was filling buckets with gravel. Another man was dumping the gravel at the edge of the stream where it could be washed for gold.

When Butler hailed them, they told him the main road went on to Sacramento City, fifty miles farther down. The other road, they said, branched off to Hangtown, six miles away, where many miners were then digging.

This was the fourth day of September.

20

"I've got to take the womenfolks to some town, and then decide where to start mining," Brush said, attempting to explain why he was standing idly by instead of rushing into the creek to dig the gold for which he had made the long journey. The others remained standing idly by, too.

"I must go to Sutter's Fort," Butler remarked and looked at Polly. "We'll have plenty of time afterward to make plans."

"I'll go along with you." This came from Hedges.

"That wad take us all to Sacramento City," was Mac-Taggart's comment.

"I'm glad we're going on together," Polly declared.

Brush started his team, and the others followed.

XXIV

JOURNEY'S END

COLIN BRUSH was pottering with hammer and saw, putting together a light frame for a tent. Under the frame he fastened poles to serve as the runners of a sled; over it he nailed some old canvas which MacTaggart had used for hundreds of miles as covering for his loaded travois. The work finished, Colin sat on the ground, his back against a tree, looking down into the dust, the bustle, and the confusion that was Sacramento City.

He had made camp among some great live oaks, as widely spaced as in a park, on rolling land over which wild oats rippled, and orange, white and purple wild flowers were scattered in single-colored beds. Below him, on the bank of a wide stream, seven or eight short streets led back from the river, and three or four longer ones crossed these at right angles. All but three of the buildings were of cotton sheeting on skeleton frames; and everywhere about them were the stumps or trees of the timbered bottom lands.

Beyond the trees, through the dust that hovered over the town, Colin could see a number of small ships and many small boats that were moored to the oaks along the bank. After watching for a while, he drowsed, dozed off, and wakened suddenly, surprised to find that he had been asleep.

"You say something to me?" he inquired, looking up at MacTaggart, who was leading the donkey past him.

"Ay," Jamie answered. "Did I hear you say you wad sell your cows?"

"Yes, when I go mining."

"Milk is a dollar a quart." Jamie stated the price almost reverently.

Colin rubbed his eyes and got to his feet. He was barely interested. Somehow, nothing seemed of any great importance. "Kate and May'll freshen in the spring," he said with a yawn. "Mebby the other four will, too. That's a long time to wait."

"That, come spring, is a hundred dollars a day for milk— wi'out the use of a pick!"

Unhurriedly, MacTaggart hitched his donkey to the runnered tent, got his string of travois together, and started toward the town with all his possessions. "A hundred dollars a day!" he called back over his shoulder. "Off at the mines, you wad dig fifty dollars a day, maybe sixty. Or ill luck hae it, not a penny."

Two young women and a child were coming up from the brook that flowed placidly past the camp. Brush stared at them. The one walking ahead was picking her way daintily through the oats and wild flowers, holding the voluminous skirt of her light brown dress at each side, as if it irked her. A perky little straw-colored hat slanted forward on her head. Colin, however, was not paying any attention to the face below the hat. As she came nearer, he could see trim feet and ankles and a whish of white petticoat at each step.

The other young woman was all in blue. In some way she reminded him of the first time he had ever met Eusebia. It was odd, he thought, that the child clinging to her hand should be barefoot, though she wore a white dress with low neck and short sleeves and a broad blue sash.

"Colin," Eusebia called from behind these strangers, "you can have the brook now; we women are through with it. Here's the soap, and there's your towel and clean things laid out. We unpacked some, fixed to go down into the town."

His wife was dressed as he had often seen her in Detroit when she went up the street to market—in a neat print with a white collar fastened in front by the big cameo brooch he had given her. She had on a scoop bonnet of black straw, and she carried a basket on her arm. In that familiar costume, he could see how loosely her basque now hung on her once comely figure.

"My laws! You could knock me down with a feather!" he exclaimed. "I didn't know you girls! Whose idea was it, fixing up—yours, Sebie?"

Mrs. Brush set her lips an instant. "If we're going to live in this place, Colin Brush," she answered, "I want we should enter it looking respectable! I've laid your things out there by the brook." Go change them frayed trousers." Grinning, he went up the stream out of sight of the camp, gave himself a thorough scrubbing, and changed his clothes. Shortly afterward, he proceeded toward the town at a leisurely gait.

In the town, men, mules, and oxen were weaving noisily and in seeming confusion in the open among barrels, bales, and boxes. Brush saw native Californians, Indians, adventurers from many different states and from all over the world, even Chinese with their loose blue clothes, pigtails, and thatchlike hats. He heard the talk of miners back from the hills and of newcomers impatient to start for the diggings.

"Oh, sure there's gold," a New Yorker told him, "for the few that are lucky enough to find it; but they put in ten dollars worth of work for every dollar in dust they take out. And that's not counting the ones that don't take out anything."

The men who did most of the talking were the disappointed ones from the mining camps. Many of these were waiting for the San Francisco boats on their way back to civilization. By noon, Brush was disillusioned and disheartened.

In an open space next to a gambling house that occupied one of the three wooden buildings of the town, he noticed a display of men's clothing hung on a rope stretched between two trees. Beside one of the trees stood the tent he had made early that morning. In front of the tent five men were waiting with shirts, coats, and trousers hung over their arms. As soon as a man came out of the tent, another one would go in. All those who entered wore the worn and dirty garb of the mines, but they came out in new, though somewhat wrinkled attire.

"Hey, dig me up something a size smaller than this!" a miner called from beside the line on which perhaps a dozen suits were still hanging.

"You hae the full stock there, Mister," MacTaggart answered, busy with three customers who were paying for what they had bought.

At last all the suits disappeared from the line and only two men waited their turns to change into their new clothes. With business less brisk, Jamie leaned against a tree and chatted with Colin.

"Suit, shirt, underwear, and hat—nine ounces of gold," he said wearily to the last man to come out.

The customer poured gold dust out of a buckskin pouch onto the small scales Jamie had set on a tree stump.

"A tack of mild weather—ay?" the Scot commented, as he emptied the gold into a large-mouthed bottle.

"But a mighty long way from anywhere," the miner answered.

"Richt!" MacTaggart assented. "You came by Panama?"

"No, down the Humboldt and across the desert to the Carson," the miner told him. "Then I stumbled into luck. Took a hundred and forty-five ounces out of Hangman's Gulch in four days. That was enough. I'm bound for home."

"Down the Humboldt!" Jamie caught him up with sudden interest. "Bide a wee!" He poured some of the gold onto the scales, weighed it, and returned it to his customer. "The price to ane that come by way of the Humboldt is seven ounces," he said. "Panama gets no discount."

The lucky miner poured the dust into his pouch, patted Jamie on the shoulder, and departed.

"From thirty wagons that I purchased in a bog at Fort Kearney, I hae sold today forty-six suits, most of good Scotch cloth, only twa at less than seven ounces gold, as well as many shirts and many socks. Now to pay for the tent you made. How wad you figure the charge? Three hours' darg? One ounce of gold?"

Over Colin's face went the shadow of a smile. "A tack of mild weather, ay?" he said. "You came by Panama?"

MacTaggart looked up with a start, grinned, then shook his head sadly. "It's a bitter mortifying to me that I came around the Horn, Mr. Brush," he replied. "Wad that be half an ounce more gold I hae to pay?" He looked at Colin gravely. "We gae into pleasantries, the twa of us after the dwam of the desert! But now I hae naught to sell; and that's no pleasing."

Just at that moment, Polly and little Corinne drew near.

"What do I keek at?" Jamie exclaimed. "Fine ladies!" He stooped to look closely at the dress the child had on. "Chemises!" he cried in surprise.

" 'Sh!" Polly cautioned. "She's proud of it!"

"Why wadna she be?" Jamie answered. "A pretty bairn in' a pretty frock! It gars me to find shoes for her. She stops with me, Miss Kent, while you gae about this Sacramento City."

Polly walked on a few steps, enjoying all the sights of the busy town.

"Why, Miss Kent!" A young man spoke close beside her. "I hardly knew you! I'm Otis Dimmock."

"I remember!" Polly said. "You and Doctor Brackett had about the only other light spring wagon like mine on the plains—and ponies."

"After we quit the train, our wagon and ponies left everything else behind except the fellows with the pack trains. We got in twenty-four days ago. I'm running a boarding house and a livery stable here. Brackett's gone to the mines. Tell any Rock Islanders you meet to drop in and see me."

"We camped last night up there on the bench," Polly informed him, "the Brushes, Gale Hedges, Lieutenant Butler of the South Bend train, and Jamie MacTaggart."

"Captain Frezzell is here getting outfitted for a trip to Redding's Diggings," Dimmock continued. "Zenas Rose has gone up Bear River. They're the only ones I've heard of, except Joe Barnett and Pierre Jacquin; they're in."

"Have you heard whether Lester Lee and Freddie Dascomb have come through? They were going by way of the Truckee."

"Say!" Dimmock exclaimed. "That's bad! They have to wade through miles of alkali ash half up to their knees. Old-timers here have been sending out rescue parties. They say it's terrible what they find there, ten times worse than the Carson. Hardly anyone left alive to bring in."

"The Carson was bad enough," Polly said. "Bill Murillo died there."

"No!" Dimmock shook his head and waited for the dust from passing pack trains to settle. Then he turned to hurry away, saying in a very low voice, "Poor Bill! Miss Kent, I'll run up and see you."

As Polly explored the town, she became more and more aware that everywhere the men were turning to stare at her, so she went back and stood for a time with Mrs. Brush and Ann. Eusebia was looking at some blue and white dishes a Chinese had for sale in a tent.

"I like just to look at 'em," she sighed, when Polly grew weary of waiting. "I'm so tired of tin! And I want to get my feet under my own table again! And stop eating like heathen!"

The women were back at the camp when Brush and Mac-Taggart drove the ponies up, the donkey behind them dragging the tent which had served as a dressing room and was now to be a house for Corinne.

"Mrs. Brush," Jamie said, "I hae brought ten pounds of elk steak."

"At a dollar a pound," Brush added. He called to Polly, "You can make your fortune here just hunting and selling the meat."

A rather good-looking young man whom nobody knew came into the camp just then. He was well dressed, clean shaven, and his hair was trimmed. He tossed a bundle into one of the wagons, then stared at the vision in blue that was Ann, walked over to her, and put his arm about her waist. The girl quickly tore herself away from his grasp.

"Why, Ann!" he cried, in feigned surprise but grinning mischievously. "Don't you like me without a beard?"

"Gale!" Ann exclaimed, her eyes filling with tears. "I can't believe it's you! I don't believe it yet!"

Everywhere Polly went, the men turned to stare at her.

A short time afterwards, Lieutenant Butler, barbered and soldierly neat in a trim, well-tailored suit, came stalking through the wild oats. He was followed by a dozen almost naked adult Indians and several Indian children, all of whom remained waiting in a huddled group a few steps away.

These Indians were squat and swarthy, with big heads, little beady eyes, and low foreheads. Their jet-black hair was cut all the way around on a level with their chins and bushed far out beyond their faces.

Butler stopped and stared when he saw Polly. Laughter from the others broke his spell. To hide his surge of feeling, he took her hand, bent low over it, and kissed it.

"Polly," he said, quickly, "you're right, land is the only thing in this country that's cheap—land and the labor of Indians. You wanted land. Well, I've agreed to buy a thousand acres if you like the place. It's near enough so we can live there and I can practice law in Sacramento City. These people are to work for us, and we're lucky to have them."

The girl, as well as all those around her, stared at the strange group a short distance away. "Have you seen the land?" she asked at last.

"Yes, it's just like this. High and rolling, with plenty of water and trees and a beautiful view. Captain Sutter has turned his fort into a miners' trading post. These Indians worked for him a long time; he says they are industrious as long as someone keeps constantly nagging at them and will never leave us if we treat them right. He has most of the tribe at his farm on Feather River."

"Your land — is there hay on it?" MacTaggart asked interestedly.

"Two or three hundred acres of it standing cured," Butler answered.

"Here is business!" cried Jamie. "Hay! Say, Mr. Butler, I'll pay sixty dollars a ton, as it stands, uncut. I will buy Sacramento City lots where the road comes down from the mines. Mr. Brush and Mr. Hedges will cut the hay and draw it into town in their wagons. I will sell it—twenty-five cents a pound the price is now. Twenty-five cents a pound counts to five hundred dollars a ton."

"Five hundred dollars!" Brush exclaimed.

"The men that own the pack trains curse all the time because there is no hay. Every day they would like to buy two or three tons. And off runs everybody to the mines!"

"MacTaggart, that does sound like business," Butler answered. "I'll sell you all the hay you'll need, but you'll have to come and take it. The Indians will be busy every minute till the rainy season, getting the buildings up."

"Husted Butler—attorney at law!" Jamie sat planning the future. "MacTaggart, Brush, and Hedges—hay! Sometime hay and . . . but that waits!"

Colin and Gale, both suddenly tense with interest, met his glance and nodded.

"But when'll I ever have time to find gold?" Brush mourned.

"Six cows, and milk a dollar a quart! Hay, and a wagon to draw it! Hae you no witting that is to find gold?" MacTaggart asked.

"Two other things," Butler added, after a pause. "Word has come to the fort that a man who staggered into Hangman's Gulch a few days ago with nothing but the pack on his back has struck it rich in what was thought to be a worked-out riffle, which had been abandoned. His name is William Brazos."

There was a long silence. The girls gazed at each other wide-eyed, startled by the vivid memory they shared of Abbie Brazos and her baby. Eusebia turned so that no one could see her face.

Polly spoke at last. "Two things, you said. What's the other one?"

Butler took her hand. "That double wedding tomorrow," he replied as he held her hand fast in his and smiled at Gale and Ann. "I've arranged for it at the fort. Everything will be just as you girls wanted."

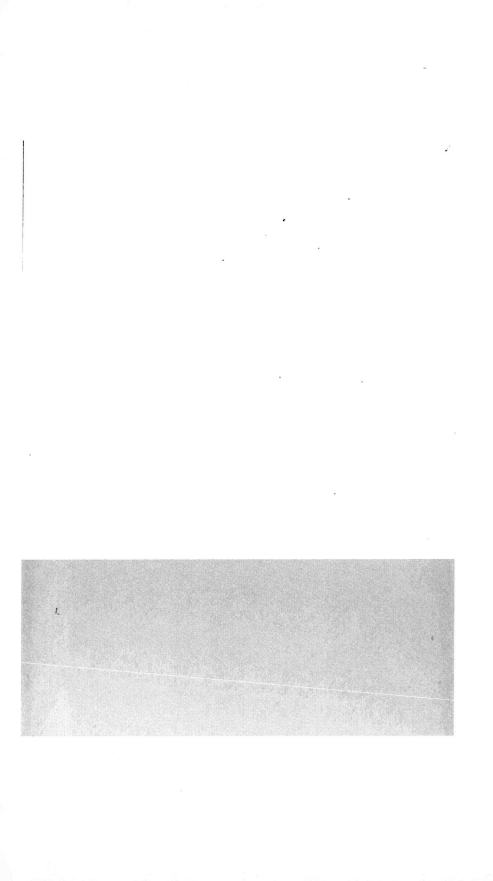

CPSIA information can be obtained
at www.ICGtesting.com
Printed in the USA
BVHW040536040122
625371BV00005B/373

9 781014 171740